WOMEN AT CORNELL
The Myth of Equal Education

WOMEN AT CORNELL

 The Myth of Equal Education

CHARLOTTE WILLIAMS CONABLE

CORNELL UNIVERSITY PRESS | *Ithaca and London*

First published 1977 by Cornell University Press.
Published in the United Kingdom by Cornell University Press Ltd., 2-4 Brook Street, London W1Y 1AA.
First printing Cornell Paperbacks 1977

International Standard Book Number (cloth) 0-8014-1098-3
International Standard Book Number (paper) 0-8014-9167-3
Library of Congress Catalog Card Number 77-3117
Printed in the United States of America by Vail-Ballou Press, Inc.
Librarians: Library of Congress cataloging information
appears on the last page of the book.

Contents

Preface

In nineteenth-century America, the suggestion that students of both sexes should attend classes together in colleges and universities incited lively debate. Coeducation, a particularly American innovation in higher education, was considered by many to be an experiment fraught with peril to women, men, and educational institutions.

Despite this intense controversy, the founders of Cornell University were firmly convinced of the value of equal education for men and women. In the century since women were first admitted to Cornell, many more coeducational colleges and universities have been established and single-sex institutions have been integrated. The principle of coeducation appears to be widely accepted.

The concept of coeducation implies not only similarity in education but also equality of educational opportunity without regard to sex. As the status of women in American society is continually being evaluated, this implication of equality in education is often used to defend the status quo. It is frequently argued that, through coeducation, women have enjoyed equal educational opportunity in this country for many years, and that if great female scientists, statesmen, and intellectuals have not developed, the fault must lie in the inadequacies of women, not in the educational system. Yet the history of women at one institution, Cornell University, shows that the policies of the administration

changed and were determined more by economic consider-
ations and social pressures than by the founders' ideals.
These changes differentiated the educational experience offered to women from that of men and resulted in dissimilar
preparation and motivation for later endeavors.

An encounter with a woman student at Cornell University about six years ago focused my attention on the relationship between the coeducational system and the role of
women in our society. The student, a determined feminist,
proclaimed in no uncertain terms that Cornell University
was one of many social institutions which oppressed
women, and she said, "Cornell has produced no worthwhile women graduates." As a loyal alumna, I was incensed
by her statement for I had not felt at all oppressed as an undergraduate, nor had any of my college contemporaries appeared unhappy or discontented. At the same time, I realized that I had no factual evidence to refute this charge of
oppression or to disprove her contention that the women
graduates had accomplished little in later life.

The outspoken young woman had challenged many of my
comfortable assumptions, and in anger I determined to
search the records of this institution for convincing evidence that she was wrong. The fact that I had no ready
response to her provocative remark demonstrated the obvious need for research into the history of women at this university. The quest for information about Cornell's women
rapidly evolved into a project of increasing complexity as
other issues emerged to be investigated and apparent para-
doxes to be resolved.

First, there was ample documentation of progressive efforts to provide higher education for women. Cornell University had been, in fact, a notable pioneer in women's education. It was the first major institution in the eastern
United States to admit women along with men (1872), to establish scholarships specifically for women (1884), to award
the Doctor of Science degree to a woman in the United
States (1895), to develop an innovative educational program

for married women through reading courses for farmers'
wives (1900), and to establish a state-supported College of
Home Economics (1925).

But these liberal efforts to educate women along with
men had failed to win the approval of young women caught
up in the contemporary feminist movement. In addition,
leading authorities on women's education challenged the
motivation of this seeming progressivism. Thomas Woody
and Mabel Newcomer sought to demonstrate that economic
motivation has been an important factor encouraging the
development of education for women. They cited Cornell
University, among others, as an example of an institution
that refused to admit women until funds were contributed
specifically for women's education.[1] It was, according to
their analyses, an institution where women were forced "to
buy their way in." Recent feminist critics of higher education repeat this charge that the university admitted women
only reluctantly as an expedient economic measure. Others
point to Cornell's status as a quasi-public institution, a condition that compelled the admission of a few "token"
women.[2]

Because the forces motivating the adoption of coeducation at Cornell are so frequently questioned, it became
necessary to explore the origins of coeducation. The commitment of the university to women as well as men can be
analyzed and understood only when placed in the proper
context. This includes the social climate of the nineteenth
century, particularly in central New York State, as well as
the goals of those individuals who established the university and shaped its special mission in higher education.

Second, the identification of "worthwhile" women graduates proved to be a difficult task, dependent upon personal
interpretations of the merit of female work. Cornell has
clearly contributed to the education of many women who
fulfilled their social mission within the home as wives and
mothers. Such women have provided a variety of useful services in "woman's place" with dedication and competence.

Others utilized their education for work outside the home, surmounted the barriers intended to exclude them because of their sex, and succeeded in professions traditionally reserved for men. Any university would be proud to count among its graduates Emily Dunning Barringer '97, M.D. '01—the first woman to win an internship at any New York City hospital and to serve on New York's horse-drawn ambulance service—who became an acknowledged leader among women in medicine. Nora Stanton Blatch, the granddaughter of one of the original advocates of women's rights, Elizabeth Cady Stanton, became in 1905 the first woman to earn a degree in civil engineering at Cornell. While much of her attention was devoted to the movement for woman suffrage, Blatch's career as an architect and developer of commercial and residential properties spanned almost half a century. Mary H. Donlon, LL.B. '20, was outstanding as an undergraduate, as the editor of the Cornell Law School journal, and later as one of the few women appointed to a federal judgeship.

Cornell women have been recognized for their outstanding professional achievements. Alice C. Evans, a graduate of Cornell's College of Agriculture in 1909, became a bacteriologist, and her research identifying the organism that causes undulant fever in humans was hailed as one of the most important medical advances in the first quarter of this century. The only American woman to win the Nobel Prize in literature and a recipient of a Pulitzer Prize as well, Pearl S. Buck received a master's degree in English from Cornell in 1925. Barbara McClintock, Ph.D. '27, received all her training as a geneticist at Cornell and in 1970 was awarded the National Medal of Science.

While alumnae assumed traditional roles as wives and mothers throughout university history, a disproportionate number of women who excelled in nontraditional roles and the university's innovative programs on behalf of women appeared to be concentrated in the first half-century of the institution's history. The pioneering women and programs seemed to become less numerous as the university grew in size, professional orientation, and reputation.

In later years, another distinctive group of alumnae, members of the post–World War II generation, emerged as leading activists in the women's movement of the 1960s and later years. These women, sensitive to issues of equity related to their sex, were among those who led the criticism of male-oriented institutions. For example, Barbara B. Bergmann '48, professor of economics at the University of Maryland, is a recognized authority on the economic impact of discrimination against women and a member of the National Commission for International Women's Year. Ruth Bader Ginsburg '54, the first woman member of the faculty of the Columbia University Law School, and Judith W. Younger '54, the first woman in the administration of the Cornell University Law School, are prominent authorities on the legal aspects of sex discrimination. Susan Brownmiller '56, one of the founders of a radical feminist group in New York City, is the author of the widely acclaimed study *Against Our Will: Men, Women and Rape.* As a member of the New York State Assembly, Constance E. Cook '41, LL.B. '43, was a leading advocate of abortion reform legislation and, as a member of Cornell's Board of Trustees, was chairman of the committee that evaluated the status of women at Cornell.

The study of women's history reveals a pattern of development which is cyclical in nature rather than evolutionary.[3] Relative to the developmental patterns of men, the proportion of women who sought a college degree, graduate training, and ultimately nontraditional social roles increased from the late nineteenth century until the 1930s, then declined until 1950, and recently has again increased. This pattern appears also in the history of women at Cornell.

Historically, such shifting patterns result from the interaction of social, political, and economic forces. Because I wanted to understand this pattern of change in a single institution, a university, the second area of my concern became the influence of Cornell upon its women students in terms of their self-image and personal goals. I sought to determine whether similar educational experiences had indeed been constantly provided for both sexes through the years. The answer to this question required an examination of institutional policies.

Although Cornell was a pioneer in the education of women, it cannot serve as a model since it is a uniquely structured combination of private colleges, such as Arts and Sciences, Engineering, Architecture, and Law, along with colleges supported by the State of New York: Human Ecology, Agriculture, Industrial and Labor Relations, and Veterinary Medicine. The university functions as the land grant college of the state while it also maintains studies in the humanities and professions. This institution, nevertheless, by its very complexity, provides an unusually broad perspective on the place of women in higher education and the important influence of university policy on the female educational experience.

In this investigation, various methods of research have been employed. Certainly personal experiences as an undergraduate and as an alumna of twenty-six years provide a basic frame of reference. Interviews and correspondence with Cornellians who were connected with the university at various periods, as well as with faculty and staff, have been very productive. The Archives of Cornell University, university documents, newspapers, periodicals, and alumnae and registrar's records have been fruitful sources of information. The many books already written about Cornell and Cornellians have provided much source material, but none has dealt specifically with the education of women. I have made every effort to use only information available to me as an interested alumna and not to violate the confidentiality implicit in my service as a member of the Board of Trustees. The collection of data was for the most part completed before I was elected trustee.

My original intent was to focus on the women of Cornell, their experiences as students, and their reactions in later life to the impact of their education. To obtain some impressionistic evidence from alumnae, a survey was conducted by mail in 1972 of sixty-one women, of whom forty-three responded. As the study evolved from an analysis of women graduates into an examination of the historical background of coeducation and the university policies affecting the female experience, this survey proved to be too limited in conception to provide more than supplementary evidence. The information supplied by these specially selected women is, however, useful as enrichment to the major investigation. Therefore, the criterion of selection and a sample of the responses are included as an appendix.

Any book about women presents a special dilemma for the author. It is difficult to determine a standard form for names. An illustration of the dimensions of this problem is found in a letter from Mary S. Jaffe '37 to me concerning the names used by her mother, Mollie Crawford '04, M.D. '07.

The subject of her names was complicated: socially she was perfectly happy to be Mrs. Edward Schuster, and legally, Mary Crawford Schuster (also my maiden name, causing endless confusion— once we got our driving licenses crossed—since women cannot use "Jr."); professionally she was Mary M. Crawford, M.D.; to friends of my generation, including my husband, she was "Dr. Mary"; to her contemporary relatives and friends she was "Mollie." "Dr. Schuster" was anathema. And to my many cousins (Mother was one of eight) she was "Aunt Mollie." Well, do the best you can— this is an aspect of feminine difficulties that *Ms* Magazine has not yet coped with.[4]

A career or the combination of career and marriage challenges the traditional forms of nomenclature, and women have responded in a variety of styles. A married woman may retain her own surname for professional purposes or adopt the name of her husband. Some married women use both their own and their husbands' names, while some single women combine a middle name with a surname. Di-

vorce further complicates the issue and forces another decision of which name to adopt. The case of Mary H. Donlon
'20 is unique. She was well known professionally under that
name for many years; a dormitory, scholarships, and several Cornell programs bear her name. Fifty-one years after
her graduation, she married and became Mrs. Alger. As I
was confronted with so many variations, I decided to use
the name by which the individual was generally known and
identified in published records.

Throughout the process of preparation of this book, assistance was readily available from a variety of sources. Faculty, staff, and colleagues in the Women's Studies Program
and the Continuing Education for Women Program at
George Washington University, as well as those at Cornell
University, provided invaluable guidance and encouragement. The staff of Cornell University's Department of
Manuscripts and University Archives provided rich resources of information and a most hospitable environment
for research. Also appreciated is the assistance of personnel
at the Library of Congress and the American Association of
University Women Educational Foundation Library in
Washington, D.C. Interwoven into this history are the experiences of many women and men of Cornell who contributed their time and thoughts most generously.

The probing questions and constructive comments of Lois
G. Schwoerer of George Washington University were much
needed and are deeply appreciated. Joanna S. Zangrando,
formerly of George Washington University and now at
Skidmore College, also improved this analysis with the pre-
cision and verve of her critique. I am also indebted to the
following individuals connected with Cornell University
who in various ways have been helpful to me: Frank R.
Clifford, Gould P. Colman, Ruth W. Darling, Carol B. Ep-
stein, Jennie T. Farley, Margaret Feldman, Scharlie B.
Handlan, Ruth W. Irish, G. Michael McHugh, Jane T.
McHugh, Richard M. Ramin, Ann Roscoe, Ben F. Stam-
baugh, Patricia C. Stewart, and Sheila Tobias. Lisa S.

Turner and Louise Boyle of the University Press were most generous in sharing their professional wisdom to perfect this manuscript.

A special acknowledgment must be given to my husband and four children. I am much indebted to them all for their constant support and their steadfast belief in the worth of this project.

It was Stephanie Seremetis, Class of 1972, whose provocative comments inspired this study. I hope the evidence compiled here will prove as instructive for her as the search for Cornell's women has been for me.

CHARLOTTE W. CONABLE

Washington D.C.

WOMEN AT CORNELL
The Myth of Equal Education

Prologue

> No woman who was not born before the Civil War knows
> out of what Egyptian darkness women came into the
> promised land of political equality and educational oppor-
> tunity.
>
> M. Carey Thomas

M. Carey Thomas, as a young woman, sensed the negative cultural forces limiting the role and expectations of
women. She investigated their origins and determined to
overcome them. An essential element in her plan was to obtain the same college education as men. At Cornell University, she found equal educational opportunity, was elected
to Phi Beta Kappa, and graduated in 1877. Later, her forceful leadership as president of Bryn Mawr College and her
insistence on excellence in women's education transformed
that institution into the intellectual mecca for women. At
the Fiftieth Anniversary Celebration of Bryn Mawr,
M. Carey Thomas was honored for her many achievements.
It was said that "she more than any other woman in her
generation, was responsible for the social acceptance of
higher education for her sex."[1]

As she attempted to elude the Egyptian darkness, Thomas
discovered that the forces confining women were diverse
and powerful. Foremost was the Judeo-Christian heritage,
which provided the ultimate authority on the proper sphere
for women. She thoughtfully considered the biblical ac-
counts of the curse of Eve and the concept of woman as the
wellspring of all evil. In the letters of St. Paul, she found
that women should be silent in church and never exert authority over men. Determined to ascertain for herself if the

Martha Carey Thomas entered Cornell University in 1875 determined to prove that women could excel academically. Coeducation, she found, was a "fiery ordeal" for a woman but it was the only means available at the time to prepare for serious scholarly endeavors as men did. An ardent feminist, she adopted the masculine form of her name while an undergraduate and was thereafter known as Carey. As president of Bryn Mawr College from 1894 to 1922, she required rigorous intellectual training for women students and provided an inspiring model for them. (Courtesy of the Library of Congress.)

Bible proved, as she was told, that woman was inferior, she finally concluded there was no biblical injunction which would prevent her attendance at college. Fortunately, the religious training of Carey Thomas incorporated the strong influence of a Quaker heritage in which women were regarded as the spiritual and intellectual equals of men. In contrast, the traditional morning prayer of the Orthodox Jew praised the Lord for not having him born as a gentile, a slave, or a woman.

Similar limiting concepts were imbedded in English common law, as interpreted by Blackstone's *Commentaries,* which pervaded legal thought. According to Blackstone, the married woman was one person with her husband. In practice, the person was the husband. The wife was a nonperson, with no rights to her property, her wages, or her children.

Another argument confining woman in the Egyptian darkness was biological. As the ideal of true womanhood gained currency in nineteenth-century America, the physical strength of pioneer women was obscured. Delicacy and frequent fainting spells became fashionable. It was considered opinion that women lacked sufficient physical endurance to withstand the strain of education and might suffer from it. Although little was actually known about the female brain, its quality and capacities were deemed inferior to the male brain.

Woman's body clearly defined her destiny. She was thought suited by nature to marry and bear children. The Wisconsin Supreme Court enunciated this theory with powerful clarity in 1875, declaring, "The Law of Nature destines and qualifies the female sex for the bearing and nurture of the children of our race and for the custody of the homes of the world . . . in love and honor. And all life-long callings of women, inconsistent with these radical and sacred duties of their sex . . . are . . . when voluntary, treason against it."[2] The assumptions underlying this decision elevated woman's natural function and limited the boundaries of her domestic world.

For centuries, the place of women had been clearly defined by theology, the law, and women's special biological function. Therefore, women had little need for education. In the European tradition, education was a luxury reserved for upper-class women and consisted of instruction in embroidery, French, painting, and the social graces. The purpose of educating women was effectively expressed by the French philosopher Jean-Jacques Rousseau, who said: "A woman's education must therefore be planned in relation to man. To be pleasing in his sight, to win his respect and love, to train him in childhood, to tend him in manhood, to counsel and console, to make his life pleasant and happy, these are the duties of woman for all time, and this is what she should be taught while she is young."[3]

Carey Thomas concluded that these limiting views of woman, of her ability and her role in society, were highly objectionable. There were others who shared her opinion. As early as 1697, Daniel Defoe had spoken out on behalf of education for women in his *Essays on Projects:* "I have often thought of it as one of the most barbarous customs in the world, considering us a civilized and Christian country, that we deny the advantages of learning to women. We reproach the sex every day for their folly and impertinence, which I am confident, had they the advantages of education equal to us, they would be guilty of less than ourselves."[4] His critique had little effect, however, and educational systems continued to follow the European model. Education for males included intellectual training for professional work while education for females included training in suitable domestic accomplishments.

In colonial America, the libertarian ideology of the Revolution refueled the debate on the education of women. Abigail Adams is well known for her entreaty to her husband, John, "to remember the ladies" as he formulated a new democratic government. She was convinced also that, if the new nation required heroes, statesmen, and philosophers, learned women were needed to educate these men, their sons.

In 1790, Judith Sargent Murray of Massachusetts was one of the first women to challenge publicly the inferior education provided for women. Questioning whether nature had really bestowed mental superiority on only one half of the human race, she asked: "Will it be said that the judgment of a male two years old, is more sage than that of a female of the same age? I believe the reverse is generally observed to be true. But from that period, what partiality! how is the one exalted, and the other depressed, by the contrary modes of education which are adopted! the one is taught to aspire, and the other is early confined and limited. As their years increase, the sister must be wholly domesticated, while the brother is led by the hand through all the flowery paths of science."[5]

Mary Wollstonecraft's powerful treatise, *The Vindication of the Rights of Women,* was published in 1792 in both England and the United States. With passion and persuasive power, she refuted the limitations placed on women by the law, the philosophers, and custom. She lamented the degradation and trivializing of women by traditions which reinforced the presumed superiority of men. One of the remedies she advocated was improved education for women and in a new form:

To improve both sexes they ought, not only in private families, but in public schools, be educated together. If marriage be the cement of society, mankind should all be educated after the same model, or the intercourse of the sexes will never deserve the name of fellowship, nor will women ever fulfill the peculiar duties of their sex, till they become enlightened citizens, till they become free by being enabled to earn their own subsistence, independent of men. . . . They cannot be injured by the experiment; for it is not in the power of man to render them more insignificant than they are at present.[6]

These individual voices, important as seminal forces, spoke out as part of a larger movement for human freedom and equality which was sweeping the western world. In the period preceding the Civil War, there was extensive and sustained effort to broaden the political, social, and economic rights of men. Impeded by the repressive forces of the Egyptian darkness, the rights of women were extended with far greater reluctance.

Education was important in a democratic society, and as the frontier gave way to settled communities, schools rapidly became an integral part of community life. Education for women was provided for reasons not of equity but, rather, of economy. Taxpayers who supported public education demanded admission for daughters as well as sons. In some cases, the full value of a teacher's salary could be received only by including young women in classes during the hours or seasons when young men were needed for work at home. Therefore, education for women became available as a fringe benefit of the education of men, not as the innate right of women. As the nation expanded, the educational system became more extensive and highly structured. The establishment of academies, seminaries, and public high schools created a demand for trained teachers.

The need for professional teachers, coupled with the demand for women in this field who were willing to accept lower wages than men, stimulated the expansion of higher education for women. Emma Willard and Catharine Beecher established seminaries to train teachers. Mount Holyoke College is generally considered the first women's college in the United States, founded in 1837. However, Mount Holyoke did not achieve collegiate status until 1893, long after the founding of Elmira College in 1855 and Vassar College in 1865.

There were colleges already in existence to provide professional training for prospective clergy, lawyers, and teachers but these institutions were reserved for men. Over two hundred years passed after the founding of Harvard

College in 1636 before four young women were permitted in 1837 to study along with the men of Oberlin College. The award of Bachelor of Arts degrees in 1841 to three of these women marked the first time American women received degrees comparable to those of men, and of even greater significance, the first time women had studied in the same institution with men.

Other coeducational institutions, following the lead of Oberlin, appeared in the Midwest. Several factors caused the frontier states to provide a climate conducive to the development of sexually integrated colleges. The strength of the tradition of sexual segregation in higher education so strong in the eastern United States was diminished by the migration west, educated women were in short supply to function as wives and teachers, and the economy of educating both sexes together was particularly decisive. Antioch College admitted women in 1853 and two years later Iowa established the first state university to enroll women.

Before the Civil War, isolated individuals advocated equity for women in higher education, and a few institutions did admit women. The war itself served as an effective catalyst, destroying traditional restraints and encouraging the utilization of women in new activities outside the home. The darkness that Carey Thomas had described was slowly giving way.

1 New York: The Frontier of Ideas

A full report of the women's rights agitation in the State of New York would in a measure be the history of the movement.

Elizabeth Cady Stanton, Susan B. Anthony, and Matilda J. Gage
The History of Woman Suffrage

Coeducation was adopted by various institutions in the Midwest after the Civil War, but in the eastern states the pattern set by the prestigious single sex institutions such as Harvard, Yale, and Vassar predominated. In view of the general reluctance of eastern institutions to admit women along with men, it is of particular interest that Cornell University approved the admission of women in 1872, one of the first eastern institutions to do so. Cambridge, Massachusetts, or New York City might seem more likely sites for such a significant effort to expand educational opportunities for women. Instead the coeducational model was adopted in Ithaca, a small town in central New York State. Therefore, the social forces operative in upstate New York in the nineteenth century which encouraged a wider sphere for women have special relevance to this inquiry.

In New York, a unique combination of factors enhanced the dynamism of the early nineteenth century. One of the less populated areas at the time of the Revolution, New York embraced a vast expanse of fertile wilderness which attracted settlers, and by 1820 had become the most heavily populated state in the nation. The rapid growth of population continued between 1830 and 1860 until one-seventh of the nation's inhabitants resided in this state.[1]

The development of new modes of transportation accelerated economic expansion and also induced some trauma in the region. The voyage of Robert Fulton's steamboat up the Hudson River in 1807 marked the advent of a new era in travel and trade. After 1825, the Erie Canal became a major route between the East and the virgin territories of the West. Since almost 100,000 people were traversing the state annually by 1845, the canal was a cause of social instability: it encouraged the rapid transmission of new ideas, and it prevented the development of a highly structured society.[2] Because of the area's dependence upon the canal, it was particularly vulnerable to recurring cycles of prosperity and depression. All New Yorkers, including those in Ithaca, lived in an atmosphere of constant excitement, induced by social, economic, and political ferment.

Economic growth, stimulated by the canal, had great impact upon the lives of the people. For women, the construction of textile mills along the route of the canal brought freedom from the task of producing cloth at home and also provided a source of paid employment outside the domestic sphere. The variety of products that were imported by canalboat supplanted domestically produced goods and thereby increased the amount of leisure time available to women. Men who had previously been frontiersmen and farmers became skilled laborers employed by others. The constant economic uncertainty compelled the workers to band together to secure their rights and improve their status. By 1830, the infant labor movement had spread to upstate New York and its leaders persistently urged the extension of free public education as a means of self-improvement.

Along with rapid settlement and economic expansion, the educational system did evolve as soon as communities became organized. Common schools were founded, some educating boys and girls together. Between 1820 and 1840, academies which offered education beyond the elementary level grew in number from 25 to 101.[3] Women were admitted to some of these institutions and the corresponding growth of female seminaries further expanded their opportunities.

In central New York, there were several institutions of higher education for men: Hamilton College, founded in 1793; Union College, established in 1795; and Geneva College (now Hobart College), which opened in 1822. These colleges were, for the most part, very limited in enrollment of students and in curriculum. When the future president of Cornell, Andrew Dickson White, entered Geneva College in 1849, he encountered only forty students and few committed scholars.

One of the earliest coeducational institutions in the region was the Genesee Wesleyan Seminary, which was founded in 1832 at Lima and later became Genesee College. Along with surveying, mathematics, languages, science, philosophy, and theology, this school offered drawing, painting, music, and needlework.

Education was generally regarded as essential in the development of the new republic, but the educational opportunities for women remained more severely limited than those of men. The first challenge to the common assumption that women required and were capable of learning only domestic accomplishments was mounted in New York State. Emma Willard, determined to disprove the alleged intellectual inferiority of women and also to prepare them for teaching, had already demonstrated at her seminary in Vermont that women could master the classical and scientific studies previously taught only to men.[4] New York State appeared to offer her a more promising field for the development of her efforts to provide serious education for women. Consequently, Emma Willard presented to the New York state legislature in 1819 a new plan for female education, a proposal which had to be presented in printed form because it was deemed unladylike for her to speak in public. The legislature was unmoved by her remarkable message but the city of Troy offered encouragement and financial support.

Impressed by the access the Erie Canal afforded both future students and teachers, Willard established her school in Troy in 1821. The success of her efforts can be measured by the fact that women, well trained in college-level classes, were graduated from her seminary before the first public high schools for girls and Mary Lyon's school at Mount Holyoke were opened. Preceding the establishment of normal schools, over two hundred teachers had been prepared for their profession at the Troy institution. Willard also composed some of the best textbooks available at the time. Her progressive efforts enabled women to engage in serious intellectual endeavors, the first step toward coeducation.

In this age and area of ferment, religion was another vital influence as churches were nurtured by missionaries and funds sent out from New England. Along with various other denominations, the Quakers established several communities in the Ithaca area and made a particularly positive impression since they accorded women equality within the church.

These new churches, established in the midst of a restless, economically unstable frontier society, created an environment that was highly receptive to recurrent revivalism. Other areas had similar revivals but the unusual combination of social and economic factors in upstate New York intensified their impact on this geographic area. Its susceptibility to emotionalism led to the identification of upstate New York as "the Burned-Over District."[5]

The central figure in this dramatic, widespread agitation was the itinerant preacher Charles Finney, whose intense exhortations brought thousands of sinners forward to "the anxious seat" in search of absolution and salvation. Finney's message, dedicated to the perfection of mankind and the attainment of millennial happiness, was provocative and effective. Through his ministry, the concept of sin became all-inclusive, encompassing slaveholding, intemperance, poor dietary habits, and war. Indeed, the powerful religious forces generated in upstate New York inspired social movements that soon extended far beyond the state boundaries. New Yorkers were central figures in the abolition and temperance movements in their zeal to reform society. It was in upstate New York that Mormonism was founded and the first advocates of Adventism, vegetarianism, phrenology, and spiritualism appeared. Several Utopian reform communities were formed in this environment hospitable to experimentation. The Oneida Community, founded by John Humphrey Noyes, was the most stable group and was of particular importance because Noyes advocated the restructuring of sexual relationships and equality for women.

Among those New Yorkers committed to social regeneration, one of the leaders was Gerrit Smith.[6] A man of immense wealth, Smith was more influential than others because he could provide financial support for moral crusades. All reform efforts, whether related to religion, temperance, radical abolitionism, land, peace, diet, or education, received the active support of the exemplary reformer Smith. In his manor house at Peterboro could be found fugitive slaves on their way to freedom, as well as social and political leaders engaged in heated discussions of contemporary issues.

With its origins in the egalitarianism of the frontier rather than the structured society of the eastern seaboard, the movement for social and moral reform welcomed the participation of large numbers of women. The dramatic fervor of the Finney revivals had strong appeal to women, and Finney organized them as effective assistants in his campaigns. Following their apprenticeship in the religious reform movement, the women found it a natural next step to continue their evangelism in the abolition and temperance crusades. In these movements, women became sensitized to and skilled at the politics of protest for human rights. In spite of their ardent commitment to reform efforts, women were frequently denied the opportunity for equal participation with men and this denial stimulated the formation of female antislavery societies and temperance groups. Another outgrowth of the drive for reform, the American Female Moral Reform Society was well organized in upstate New York and advocated improved education for women as a means of moral uplift.

After 1840, the tempo and vehemence of the reform movement increased. However one reacted in this controversy-laden era, it would have been extremely difficult to remain unaware that women were breaking out of their restricted domestic sphere or to ignore the singular individuals who were attracting public notice.

A native of Johnstown, Elizabeth Cady Stanton was a life-long advocate of coeducation.[7] For her, the educational experience at Emma Willard's seminary had proven barren and unstimulating because she was brilliant. Overqualified and overprepared for this school, she was denied admission to any college because she was a woman.

The cause of equal rights became her major interest. As a young woman, she had listened to the problems brought by women to her father, a judge. She learned that the law kept women in an inferior, dependent condition to live under "a defect of sex." At the home of her cousin Gerrit Smith, she was sensitized to the wide-ranging movement for radical reform.

In 1840, Elizabeth Cady married Henry Stanton, a leading abolitionist. Together they attended the World Antislavery Convention in London. At this gathering, women workers in the abolition cause were excluded from active participation because of their sex. The paradox of men meeting to consider the rights of slaves while arbitrarily excluding women infuriated Stanton and the other women. With Lucretia Mott, a Quaker minister and the first woman Stanton had ever met who believed in the equality of the sexes, she paced the streets of London and resolved to hold a meeting on the rights of women in the United States.

Returning home, Stanton joined in a petition campaign to urge the passage of a law to protect the property rights of

married women in New York. This campaign had special
significance: seldom before had a small group of women pe-
titioned on their own behalf rather than for others. When
the Married Women's Property Act was passed in 1848, it
was one of the first in the nation to recognize the right of
women to hold real estate. Stanton also began to discuss
with friends the exclusion of women from the electoral process. In advance of the constitutional convention held in
New York in 1847, she urged a few legislators to strike out
the word "male" in regard to the rights of citizens to vote
and to substitute "persons."[8] The time was not yet ripe,
however, for such liberal thought.

When Lucretia Mott visited near the Stanton home in
Seneca Falls, Elizabeth arranged a reunion. With several
other women, they discussed the social, civil, and religious
restrictions under which women were living and resolved
to hold a public meeting to discuss these issues.

Forty miles north of Ithaca in the Wesleyan Chapel in
Seneca Falls, the world's first women's rights convention
was held July 19, 1848. The Declaration of Sentiments had
been modeled upon the Declaration of Independence and
was approved by the convention delegates. Affirming the
belief that "men and women are created equal," this document set forth eighteen legal and social grievances of
women and included the first public demand for woman
suffrage. A less widely noticed but equally significant statement was also included. It specified that man had denied
woman the facilities for obtaining a thorough education,
since most colleges and universities refused to consider the
admission of women. The convention provoked a storm of
controversy and ridicule in the press. However appalled she
was by the furor, Stanton was delighted with the publicity
because, she said, "It will start women thinking, and men
too; and when men and women think about a new question, the first step in progress is taken."[9]

In the neighboring community of Geneva, another controversial event was taking place. Elizabeth Blackwell had

decided that, through medicine, she could be most useful to society.[10] She had been rejected by every major medical school in the East before gaining admission to Geneva College. Although women had been bandaging wounds and delivering babies for centuries, the idea that women could or should study medicine and become familiar with the human body was too revolutionary for most to accept. She eventually won acceptance among the faculty and students by her competence and serious purpose, but she remained a curiosity to many residents of Geneva. In January 1849, Blackwell received her degree from Geneva College—the first woman to be awarded the Doctor of Medicine degree by a recognized school of medicine. She stood first in her class.

In Syracuse, Central Medical College was opened in 1849 and encouraged the admission of women. By 1850, the second woman doctor, Lydia Folger Fowler, graduated from its new headquarters in Rochester.[11] Remaining at the college for several years, Dr. Fowler lectured on anatomy, midwifery, and the diseases of women and children; she was one of the early woman professors in an American medical school. Sarah Adamson Dolley, an 1851 graduate, became the first woman intern in the United States, serving at a hospital in Philadelphia.[12] Later, in Rochester, Dolley practiced medicine along with her husband and continued her efforts to encourage professional opportunities for women. Meanwhile, Elizabeth Blackwell was compelled to go abroad for advanced training and, discouraged in her attempts to practice medicine in New York City, she eventually opened her own infirmary for women and children in the tenement district.

That women were refusing to remain in their prescribed feminine sphere was attracting public notice. Elizabeth Stanton kept up the agitation with frequent letters to the editors of newspapers, often to Horace Greeley, editor of the *New York Tribune,* the only major paper to give the women serious, sympathetic coverage. To the editor of the *National Reformer* in Rochester, she wrote: "We did not meet to discuss fashions, customs, or dress, the rights of man or the propriety of the sexes changing positions, but simply our own inalienable rights, our duties, our true sphere. . . . There is no such thing as a sphere for sex. Every man has a different sphere, in which he may or may not shine, and it is the same with every woman, and the same woman may have a different sphere at different times."[13]

A friend in Seneca Falls, Amelia Bloomer, also publicized the women's cause.[14] A member of the Ladies' Temperance Society, she edited a temperance newpaper, the *Lily*, and soon began to convey strong opinions on women's rights. She often published articles written by Elizabeth Stanton.

The *Lily* gained national attention when it publicized the radical new style of clothing worn by a woman on the streets of Seneca Falls. Elizabeth Smith Miller, the daughter of Gerrit Smith, dared to appear publicly in a knee-length skirt and beneath that, trousers![15] She was in rebellion against the bondage implicit in women's clothing, the constrictions of whale-bone corsets and yards of fabric. Other women, Stanton among them, adopted this liberating garb. Because Amelia Bloomer advocated dress reform in her paper, the name "bloomers" was given to this revolutionary fashion which quickly attracted determined adherents and also violent opponents. The women who donned bloomers found that their clothing attracted so much adverse attention that most eventually abandoned this cause, fearing such controversy would detract from their major concerns— the political, legal, and economic rights of women.

Antoinette Brown and her family, living near Rochester, had all been converted by the enthusiastic Finney revivals but the young woman's decision to become a minister shocked them.[16] At Oberlin College, the policy of equal admissions ensured her entrance to the theological course, and the faculty approved her thesis refuting St. Paul's directive that women should maintain silence in churches. However, Oberlin denied her a student license to preach and refused to approve her graduation. Brown was a highly successful lecturer before reform groups and finally, in 1853, was ordained in a central New York church, the first woman minister of a recognized denomination in the United States. This was truly an extraordinary event, attended by Gerrit Smith and acclaimed by Horace Greeley's newspaper.

Among the teachers of New York State was Susan B. Anthony, the headmistress at the Canajoharie Academy. [17] Her career impressed indelibly upon her the fact that women teachers earned far less than men. While managing the family farm near Rochester, she met leading abolitionists and became active in their cause, as well as in the temperance movement.

In Seneca Falls in 1851, Susan Anthony was introduced to Elizabeth Stanton by their mutual friend, Amelia Bloomer. For the next fifty years, Stanton and Anthony collaborated to extend the sphere of women. Stanton, the philosopher, author, and orator, was complemented by Anthony, who organized an army of indefatigable workers across the state. Together they prepared and presented letters, petitions, speeches, and constitutional arguments to every available group and to some who wished they could avoid these two and their adherents. They seized every opportunity to drive "an entering wedge" so that women could be recognized and their rights secured.

Generally esteemed primarily as leaders of the suffrage movement, Stanton and Anthony were well aware that female equality involved far more than the right to vote. Stanton once wrote to her associate: "To my mind, our Association can not be too broad. Suffrage involves every basic principle of republican government, all our social, civil, religious, educational, and political rights. It is therefore germane to our platform to discuss every invidious distinction of sex in the college, home, trades and professions, in literature, sacred and profane, in the canon as well as the civil law." [18]

During the summer of 1851, they joined forces to influence the emerging movement to establish a college in central New York. The Mechanics Mutual Protective Association, a labor organization, intended to organize a school which would offer practical education in agriculture and mechanics for the working class. Stanton and Anthony agreed that women must be included in this new educational venture. When the organizers of the People's College gathered for a meeting in Seneca Falls, Stanton and Anthony set out to drive their entering wedge and arranged to confer with Horace Greeley, a leading advocate of the college. This was a highly significant event for it marked the initial collaboration of the two women to promote women's rights. Of equal importance is the involvement of these three individuals in the projected People's College, which was the precursor of Cornell University.

Greeley was sympathetic to the women's aim and when the People's College Association convened later in Rochester, he became their spokesman. Presenting a resolution for consideration by the organization, Greeley called attention to the fact that the current system of higher education discriminated against women by excluding them. At the People's College, he proposed that women should have the freedom to pursue any course of study or occupation for which they were qualified.[19] Few of the male proponents of the college had given much thought, if any, to the inclusion of women in their plans, and they held a lengthy, heated debate on this resolution. Supported by Greeley's prestige and his vigorous defense, the resolution was ultimately adopted. The first prospectus of the People's College, issued in December 1851, stated that the school would offer "suitable facilities for the education of Young Women, as well as Young Men: all the sciences taught in the College being as freely imparted to the former as to the latter."

The following spring, the association met again in Rochester where many opponents of coeducation participated in the discussion. There was continuing dissension over the issue of the admission of women but on this occasion Greeley and a few supporters prevailed. Meanwhile, Susan Anthony maintained close contact with Harrison Howard, one of the college organizers, and wrote to him encouragingly that the cause of equal education did have friends. She was convinced that the time had come to put into effect "such a glorious plan" as was envisioned for the People's College.[20] Howard later recalled, in a memoir, the events which transpired at the association's meeting held in Seneca Falls, October 14, 1852:

This meeting was notable for the appearance to take part in the proceedings of what was then called the Women's Rights ladies, who were at the time very unpopular. . . . Mrs. Stanton, Susan B. Anthony, Mrs. Bloomer, and others were there and some of them took part in the discussion and obtained a resolution that hereafter in the prospectus the word "suitable" should read "equal" and when we came to get the Charter, and in fact, all the laws were made to read "persons" and there is nothing in them that refers to either male or female. This was done because the "Abolitionists" insisted upon having inserted "Colored men shall have equal facilities with others to study in the University." After considerable discussion, a resolution was passed that the ladies be represented on committees thereafter.[21]

Other difficulties confronted the college's proponents. It was not easy to arouse widespread public support for the proposed program and the approval of the state legislature was needed to secure an act of incorporation. Governor Washington Hunt and several other backers of the college suggested that the proposal for the education of women would provoke much dissension among conservative legislators and might cause the defeat of the charter. It would be better, they thought, to allude only to the possibility of women's education at some indefinite time in the future. The charter that was approved by the legislature in 1853 stated, "It is contemplated that a department providing for a full and thorough scientific, as well as practical course of instruction for females, will be organized as soon as a proper and satisfactory plan can be perfected."

The People's College never did become a functioning institution due to poor leadership, financial crises, the disruption of the Civil War, and other complicating factors. The planning for it served, however, as the initial skirmish in the battle to secure equal rights for women and was a testing of Stanton's and Anthony's abilities. They had made an important, if unsuccessful, stand for an ideal—equal education for women. When Cornell University was chartered in 1865, it embodied many of the ideas implicit in the People's College proposal, and some trustees of the college, including Horace Greeley, became trustees of Cornell.

Despite this initial defeat, Elizabeth Stanton and Susan Anthony mounted a multifaceted campaign to improve the status of women. In 1854, Anthony organized a statewide campaign county by county to petition the legislature, urging the enfranchisement of women and improvements in the Married Women's Property Law. Stanton testified in support of legal protection for married women before the legislature's Joint Judiciary Committee. Precedent was shattered in 1860 when Elizabeth Stanton spoke to a joint session of the legislature on the issue of married women's legal rights: she was the first woman to appear in person to address the legislators. Speaking in favor of equality for women under the law, she proposed, as she had over the years, that the words "white male" be removed from all laws and reference made only to "persons."

These two women, dedicated to social and legal reform, were indefatigable. They continually refined their strategy, enlisted new workers in their cause, and gained increasing prominence as they articulated female demands for equity. They posed a growing threat to the established order and evoked strong opposition from those defending the traditional sphere of women. In the *Albany Register*, it was reported:

While the feminine propagandists of women's rights confined themselves to the exhibition of short petticoats and long-legged boots, and to the holding of conventions and speech-making in concert rooms, the people were disposed to be amused by them, as they are by the wit of the clown in the circus, or the performance of Punch and Judy on fair days, or the minstrelsy of gentlemen with blackened faces, on banjos, the tambourine and the bones. But the joke is becoming stale. . . . People are beginning to inquire how far public sentiment should sanction or tolerate these unsexed women, who would step out from the true sphere of the mother, the wife, and the daughter, and taking upon themselves the duties and business of men, stalk into the public gaze, and by engaging in politics, the rough controversies and trafficking of the world, upheave existing institutions, and overturn all the social relations of life.[22]

Feminists continued their attack against existing institutions. Susan Anthony, the former teacher, regularly confronted the educational establishment with demands for female equality. Originally denied the right to participate in the discussions at state teachers' conventions because of her sex, Anthony persisted until she was eventually granted the opportunity to speak. From that time on, she appeared regularly across the state to urge that all schools, colleges, and universities open their doors to women. In 1856, addressing a teachers' meeting in Troy, she suggested that women must be better served by education in order to function in a broader sphere. Furthermore, she said, "A woman needs no particular kind of education to be a wife and mother anymore than a man does to be a husband and father. A man cannot make a living out of these relations. He must fill them with something more and so must women."[23]

Meanwhile, in England John Stuart Mill and Harriet Taylor were also considering the position of women in society. Collaborators in intellectual and social reforms, and later husband and wife, they believed that society must promote the highest development of each individual, unhindered by gender-related restrictions. Learning of the women's rights conventions in America, Harriet Taylor Mill published a provocative essay in 1851 in the *Westminister Review*.

In this essay, "The Enfranchisement of Women," she rejected the idea that one half of the human race should live in forced subordination to the other and denied that the purpose of educating women was to develop charming, cultivated companions for men. If the intellectual powers of women appeared limited, it was because the female intellect was never fully stimulated by superficial education. Mill took a radical position in relation to women's education: "High mental powers in women will be but an exceptional accident, until every career is opened to them, and until they, as well as men, are educated for themselves and the world—not one sex for the other." [24]

Later works by John Stuart Mill received favorable notice on both shores of the Atlantic. As the sole male intellectual leader at this time to include sex, along with class, religion, and politics, as a source of oppression, Mill was indeed an important figure. As a member of Parliament, he introduced a measure to grant women suffrage and presented a powerful address going beyond enfranchisement to discuss full social equality for women. In *The Subjection of Women,* published in 1869, he elaborated on the social causes of women's subjugation and urged greater educational and professional opportunity. This work was greeted "with joy" by Elizabeth Stanton and reached a wide audience of intellectuals and reformers in the United States. The English philosophers were striving to loosen the intellectual and legal bonds which confined women.

In America, the Civil War was precipitating sharp social change. Women responded to the challenge of wartime exigencies in various ways. Regardless of the manner of their involvement, they were drawn increasingly beyond their traditional domestic sphere. Some who had gathered periodically for tea and needlework now met regularly to produce needed items of clothing and bandages for those at the front: they worked with a sense of high purpose at necessary tasks. In Ithaca, as in other communities, women made gloves, socks, mittens, and undergarments together in a central location outside their homes. This association for war-relief activities led after the war to the development of a women's club, the Ladies Union Benevolent Society, one of the earliest women's organizations in the town.

During the war, women's rights activities were suspended, but Stanton and Anthony could not resign themselves to rolling bandages and collecting relief supplies. They saw the war as a conflict between slavery and freedom: the issue was freedom. They organized the Women's Loyal League and sent out their own army of women to circulate petitions which urged passage of the Thirteenth Amendment. The success of their efforts in New York State, already sensitive to reform, is measured by the fact that more signatures were collected in this state than in any other.

Some women, determined to be active participants in the national conflict, ventured far beyond the feminine sphere. Flamboyant Mary Walker was a native of Oswego, a graduate of the Syracuse Medical College, and a lifelong advocate of dress reform.[25] Attired as she usually was in male clothing, Walker volunteered for war service and worked as a surgeon. She was captured behind Confederate lines as she cared for sick civilians, served four months in a Rebel prison near Richmond, Virginia, and was eventually freed in an exchange of Confederate prisoners. For her wartime efforts, Mary Walker was awarded the Congressional Medal of Honor, the first woman to be so honored.

The daughter of wealthy Quakers, Emily Howland matured in Sherwood, a village twenty-two miles north of Ithaca, where her home was a station on the Underground Railroad.[26] Fired with abolitionist enthusiasm, this young woman volunteered to become a teacher in a school for free black girls in Washington, D.C. Following issuance of the Emancipation Proclamation, she organized and taught in schools in the freedmen's camps, one of which was located on the grounds of Robert E. Lee's estate at Arlington. Dedicated to alleviating the plight of the downtrodden, Howland's advocacy of education for black people continued throughout her long life. She also collaborated with Stanton, Anthony, and others who were committed to securing equal rights for women.

Long before 1872 when women achieved the right to equal education at Cornell University in Ithaca, the message, inspired in New York by New Yorkers, was clear. Some women, as well as some men, wanted all women to be free from their traditional bondage and to have equal rights with men. Some women had proven their ability to perform other than domestic work, others had become proficient at mobilizing large scale campaigns on their own behalf, and all played an important part in producing a more favorable social climate for women in New York. These activists demanded educational equity as the keystone of their campaign for women's independence.

2 The Founders: Male and Female

> I would found an institution where any person can find instruction in any study.
>
> Cornell University Motto

"Brown is agitating the question of admitting female students," the student newspaper, the *Cornell Era,* reported in 1871. "Unluckily this pride of 'Little Rhody' has no motto which decides for her the matter as conclusively as does 'I would found . . . ' decides for us."[1]

The admission of women to Cornell University is closely linked, according to legend, to the phrasing of the university motto. Campus lore alleges that the admission of women students was an accident, the result of the ambiguity of this motto. To determine whether coeducation is the result of unclear wording or clear intent, the individuals who were involved in the founding of the university must be examined. Certainly, this liberal venture—some considered it radical—was made possible, as we have seen, by the climate of social reform and by the militant feminists of New York State. Not everyone reacted positively to the reformers' efforts: in fact, many people reacted negatively and sometimes violently. Why, then, did those individuals who were responsible for defining the goals of Cornell University become participants in this controversial experiment?

Three men are traditionally regarded as the pivotal figures in the drama of the development of Cornell University: Ezra Cornell, the founder; Andrew Dickson White, the first president; and Henry Williams Sage, a member of the Board of Trustees and a major benefactor. Their involvement in this enterprise was the culmination of each man's life experiences and their shared commitment to higher education.

Ezra Cornell, attracted to Ithaca by the promise of prosperity following the route of the Erie Canal, arrived on foot in 1828. Pausing on the brow of East Hill, he stood upon land that would later provide one of the most spectacular natural sites of any university in America, and he savored the magnificent view over the village of Ithaca to the green-rimmed valley and the steely blue of Lake Cayuga. Rugged and gaunt, Cornell came armed with staunch Quaker beliefs, the equivalent of a fifth-grade education, and considerable mechanical aptitude developed during his youth on a nearby farm.

Work as a carpenter and manager of a plaster mill occupied him for several years, and then he set out on foot to peddle a new type of plow. A chance encounter with an old friend led to his eventual involvement in the construction of a new system of communication—the telegraph. The years between 1845 and 1856, when the telegraph companies merged to form the Western Union Company, had for Cornell a frustrating tempo of arduous work, fierce competition over telegraph rights, and constant indebtedness. After giving up his interest in the telegraph, he became the largest stockholder in the Western Union Company and returned home where he purchased the hilltop farm from which he had first looked out over Ithaca.

As the value of his Western Union holdings rapidly increased, Cornell was able to repay his debts, and by 1864 he had an annual income exceeding $100,000. In the Quaker tradition, Cornell wanted to provide for his family adequately but not extravagantly. Considering himself only the trustee of the great sums now available to him, he began to evaluate ways to use his wealth to benefit society.

To suggest that Ezra Cornell was an illiterate man with money, as his critics claimed, does him a grave injustice. Cornell was representative of his era, a man who could and did rise by his own efforts. He was curious about all aspects of his world and was determined to master them. His expanding interests and the vast improvement in grammar, spelling, and composition in the lengthy, descriptive letters he sent home bear witness to his successful self-education. Sensitive all his life to his own academic deficiencies, Cornell determined to open educational opportunities for others.

Of greatest concern to him were those who were generally not served by the existing educational system—farmers and industrial workers. From his own experience, he knew they required practical training and scientific information. Cornell organized farmers' clubs, provided the facilities for an agricultural reading room, and became one of the leading advocates of a state agricultural college in the area. His first major philanthropy was the endowment of a free public library for the citizens of Ithaca.

Cornell's vote, as a member of the New York State Assembly, to approve the charter of Vassar College indicates his awareness of the contemporary campaign to expand the traditional sphere of women and his support for their entry into higher education. Two of his daughters became students at Vassar. In addition, Cornell was well aware that women were entering the labor force in increasing numbers for he had participated in the opening of a new occupation for women through the development of the telegraph. In this untested, unstable industry, it soon became evident that women were more desirable than men as telegraph operators because not only were women willing to accept lower wages than men but also, during the frequent slack periods of operation, they could occupy themselves with knitting and sewing. Cornell's sister Phoebe was one of the early women telegraphers, serving in the Albion, Michigan, office.

Supportive of women's efforts to become students and workers, Ezra Cornell also envisioned a place for women in the field of medicine. His frequent illnesses and the deaths of four of his children convinced him of the great need for improved medical care. Cornell decided to establish a water cure sanitarium in Ithaca and at the suggestion of Dr. Samantha Nivison (who lived nearby and was one of the early graduates of the Female Medical College in Philadelphia), he included in his plans a medical course to train women as physicians and nurses. A fund drive was initiated and construction started on a large stone structure overlooking Cascadilla Gorge. Dr. Elizabeth Blackwell, hearing of Cornell's project, wrote to explore their "strong mutual interest in a noble cause." [2] She was attempting to raise funds to build a medical school for women in connection with her New York Infirmary for Women and Children. But Cornell encountered difficulties in developing this new institution and had to respond that, under the circumstances, he hoped in the future to establish a medical school to which women would be admitted along with men. [3] Cornell also contributed a scholarship to the New York Medical College for Women, the first women's medical school in the state.

In any consideration of Ezra Cornell's interest in the education of women, his wife, Mary Ann, must be seen as a decisive influence. Like her husband, Mary Ann had little formal education. One of two daughters in a family of eleven children, she and her sister attended the district school on alternate weeks so that one girl could always be home to help with domestic chores. The Cornells' marriage in 1831 had precipitated his excommunication from Quaker meeting because Mary Ann was an Episcopalian. Ezra rejected the opportunity for reinstatement, convinced that the marriage was one of the wisest things he had ever done, and refused to humiliate his wife publicly by confessing regret for this action.

For at least fifteen years while Cornell was often away attempting to develop his telegraph company, Mary Ann stayed at home with an increasing number of children, a modest farm, some cows, pigs, and sheep, rent from a few tenants, and little else. There were long periods when her husband had no money for himself nor any to share with her. Fortunately, Mary Ann's father was confident that his son-in-law would ultimately succeed and often visited the family with a wagon filled with provisions. By the time she was forty years old, Mary Ann Cornell had borne nine children, seen four die, and had acquired grey hair and false teeth. Despite the loneliness and rigors of their lengthy separations, the correspondence between husband and wife reflects sincere mutual concern and deep devotion.[4]

Mary Ann Cornell: "The wife to whose efforts and privations and struggles that institution owes its existence, as much as to the founder himself."— Ezra Cornell. (Cornell University, DMUA.)

Cornell knew that the plight of his wife, a woman with children dependent upon others for economic support, was a common problem. During the Civil War, the Cornells were actively involved in community efforts to provide supplies for those at the war front and also for the families who were left behind at home. They saw the desperate problems of survival that many Ithaca women confronted when husbands went off to war and often did not return. Cornell offered to contribute $1,000 to the Ithaca women's war-relief organization if they would provide means of employment for soldiers' wives and other women who needed a source of support for themselves and their families. This perceptive humanitarian realized that women were severely handicapped by the limited opportunities available to them for education and employment, and he determined that women must be included in future educational ventures.

When plans were underway for the establishment of Cornell University, Ezra and Mary Ann went to the top of East Hill to study the area where the first building was to be located. He scooped up the first shovelful of dirt in the long history of university construction and she, the second. This special soil, jointly broken, symbolized for them mutual effort and sacrifice. Later, Ezra Cornell paid tribute to his wife with a letter in which he recalled their many years of hardship and separation. He noted also the many honors which had come to them, and for Mary Ann, he thought being "the wife to whose effort and privations and struggles that institution owes its existence, as much as to the founder himself . . . is an honor higher and nobler than falls to the lot of many women." Cornell then suggested that Mary Ann should consider "founding a system of industry" so that young women of limited means, similar to her own economic situation at the time of their marriage, could earn the funds necessary to secure an education at Cornell University. In Ezra Cornell's opinion, educational opportunity and economic independence would prove to be far more important for women than the right to vote.[5]

Ezra Cornell's views on the education of women were the result of his personal experience with educational and economic deprivation: those of Andrew D. White evolved in quite different circumstances. Unlike Cornell, White had not worked his way out of poverty but was a member of a wealthy and distinguished central New York family. Whereas Cornell's education was limited, White's was exceptional for the time.

White attended Geneva College for one year, during which he found himself unhappily out of place, an eager scholar in the midst of playful boys who had limited academic motivation. Depressed by the aridity of this environment, he found solace in the library reading about English universities which seemed to him intellectually and visually exciting. He began to dream of establishing his own ideal university, complete with quadrangles, libraries, and majestic buildings overlooking one of New York's Finger Lakes. This vision persisted in later years and became more elaborate with time and experience.

In 1853, the youthful White graduated with honors from Yale University, then traveled and studied abroad, and eventually earned a master's degree at Yale. White had found many deficiencies in his American education, but he was inspired by the intellectual excitement generated in European universities. His career as an academic reformer was well underway when, as a professor at the University of Michigan, he began to experiment with his own educational theories.

That Andrew D. White espoused liberal causes is not surprising. He had grown up in Syracuse, which because of its central location in the state was the vortex of the intense reform movements that swept across New York. He was accustomed to attending meetings and hearing debates on current issues. The notable reformers of the period were his acquaintances. To him, advocacy of social change was a normal part of existence.

Of all the public figures White came to know, he considered Gerrit Smith the most admirable. Many people thought Smith a fanatic, but White saw him as an enlightened leader of social and moral reform, a man of integrity, and one who was willing to contribute funds generously in support of his views. Among the various causes encouraged by Smith, the campaign for women's rights was a major interest, as it was to his relative and ally, Elizabeth Cady Stanton.

As an associate of Gerrit Smith, the Reverend Samuel J. May was also highly regarded by White. May, a Unitarian minister in Syracuse, devoted his life to a fearless personal crusade for equal rights. He had, on occasion, been stoned by mobs and hanged in effigy because of his controversial involvement in the abolition movement. When May preached his first sermon on the rights of women in 1846, however, it was so well received that his message was published both in the United States and England.

From Samuel May, White received spiritual inspiration and a sensitivity to radical reform; in addition he received a more tangible gift—a fine portrait of Prudence Crandall, which White had long admired in May's home. May had supported the efforts of Prudence Crandall to teach black as well as white girls in her school, an endeavor that aroused the wrath of the community, inspired violent opposition, and ultimately failed. The portrait of this early warrior in the long struggle for equal rights had been presented to May as a token of appreciation for his assistance, and May in turn promised the painting to White when the admission of women had been accomplished at Cornell University.[6]

Certainly White's determination to include women in his educational reforms was encouraged by the women in his family. He attributed his interest in the education of women to his mother, Clara Dickson White, who was a strong influence throughout his life. She was not persuaded of the merit of some of her son's reforms but she was convinced that both sexes could derive equal benefits from education. Remembering her own experience at the Cortland Academy, she told him, "The young men and young women learned to respect each other, not merely for physical, but for intellectual and moral qualities; so there came a healthful emulation in study, the men becoming more manly and the women more womanly; and never, so far as I have heard, did any of the evil consequences follow which some of your opponents are prophesying."[7]

For many years, White was devoted to his wife, Mary, a

woman of intelligence, charm, and personal warmth. A well-educated woman for her time, Mary White had studied at Miss Bradbury's school in Syracuse and later developed her musical talents through lessons in New York City. Her influence was vital in the life of her scholarly husband. When Mary died suddenly, White paid tribute to the importance of "her thoughtful counsel and loving confidence" during the most difficult years of his life.[8] He later remarried but White marked the anniversary of Mary's death with a cross in his diary each year until his own death in 1918.[9] Mary White, through her own life, had provided convincing evidence of the benefits of education for women.

Upon the death of his father, White inherited $300,000 and was at last able to consider implementing his dream of founding a radically different educational institution. Realizing that his inheritance was insufficient for his purposes, White, at the urging of Samuel May, wrote to Gerrit Smith in 1862 to enlist Smith's aid. In this letter, White described in great detail his own conception of "a truly great university." A primary objective would be, he wrote,

First, to secure a place where the most highly prized instruction may be afforded to all—regardless of sex or color. . . . To admit women and colored persons into a petty college would do no good to the individuals concerned; but to admit them to a great university would be a blessing to the whole colored race and the whole female sex—for the weaker colleges would be finally compelled to adopt the system.[10]

To his great disappointment, White found that Smith was unwilling to join in this endeavor. The realization of his ambitious plan was not abandoned, however, but was only postponed until White could identify other suitably sympathetic collaborators.

The mutuality of interest between Ezra Cornell and Andrew D. White became apparent after 1864 when both served in the New York State Senate. White was impressed by Cornell's plans to endow a public library in Ithaca and also the sanitarium, which included a proposal for women's medical education. He admired a man who was using his wealth constructively and was interested in educational opportunities for women. Cornell respected the younger man's intellectual attainments and sought his advice on the most urgent social needs in which the telegraph profits could be most beneficially invested. They explored together various possibilities and soon discovered many areas of agreement about the deficiencies of higher education. As the two men were considering informally the desirability of founding an institution, the state legislature became embroiled in a bitter dispute over the disposition of the federal funding made available under the Morrill Land Grant Act. Passed in 1862, this act was designed to encourage the states to establish agricultural and technical colleges. In New York State, the Morrill Act became the focus of extensive controversy: at least twenty denominational colleges were eager to share in the Morrill bounties. Cornell and White originally supported opposing institutions in this struggle, but they eventually joined forces to secure the entire land grant allotment for one institution, their university.[11]

There can be no question that the education of women along with men was precisely what Cornell and White were dedicated to accomplishing at their university. It was Ezra Cornell who reputedly expressed the sentiments reflected in the university motto—that his institution was intended for any "persons." Andrew D. White, however, prepared university legislation for consideration by the state legislators. He realized that securing a favorable vote was a complex problem since Cornell University had already aroused strong opposition. Some people resented the fact that the university would receive all the land grant funds, and others objected to the radical nature of the secular, practical education to be offered at Cornell. In addition, Ezra Cornell was under continual personal attack as a rich man who was attempting to acquire greater wealth through use of the land grant funds. White was fearful that more support from the conservative legislators would be lost by injecting the provocative issue of coeducation into the debate. Therefore, he laid the groundwork for future action by deliberately selecting the word "person" instead of "man" for all legislation pertaining to Cornell University.[12] The legislature did approve the university charter in 1865.

Now confronted with the practical problems of founding an institution, Andrew D. White devoted his efforts to educational plans while Ezra Cornell sought the means to develop a sound financial base for the university. The third man involved in the history of coeducation at Cornell, Henry Sage, was consulted by Cornell about suitable areas of investment for university funds. Sage, a prototype of the self-made, wealthy Victorian businessman, had developed a reputation for skill and shrewdness in the course of his business career. Once thus involved as financial consultant, Henry Sage played a far more decisive part in university development than is generally recognized.[13]

Sage and his family moved to Ithaca in 1827, drawn by the same lure of prosperity that had attracted Ezra Cornell, but the promising prospects soon evaporated when his father was unable to find steady employment, and the family was plagued by illness and lack of funds. Young Henry was forced to abandon his ambition to attend Yale University, and except for occasional scientific classes in Ithaca, his formal education was at an end. Finally, his father deserted the family, leaving Henry with complete responsibility for his mother and sisters.

The experiences of these early years affected Sage deeply. Poor, uneducated, and disgraced, he became determined to prove himself. The emotional optimism of the Finney revivals and the doctrine of salvation through good works supported Sage's ambition and his drive for self-affirmation. Like Ezra Cornell, his own limited academic experience sensitized Sage to the significance of education in personal development. In his diary, he noted, "My early education was slight and improperly conducted. . . . Now I begin to feel the need of it and to feel that every earthly thing is worthless and useless compared with knowledge." [14] Throughout his life, Sage was a voracious reader. interested in a variety of subjects. To Henry Sage, education was the key to self-improvement and social betterment.

Starting as a store clerk, Sage eventually became involved in the burgeoning lumber trade. Following the Civil War, he formed a partnership with John McGraw to establish one of the major lumber mills in the Saginaw Valley of Michigan. Through his widespread lumbering ventures, Sage became a wealthy man, a skilled administrator, and a man accustomed to the exercise of power.

Sage moved to Brooklyn in 1857 in order to be closer to the center of business activities. For the next twenty years, he was an active member and lay leader of Henry Ward Beecher's church, a major center of liberalism. Beecher had long been a prominent leader and stirring orator in contemporary reform movements, particularly the campaign for equal rights for women. To Sage, Beecher exemplified Christian virtue and noble activism for social justice. He was also a highly regarded friend. Sage invested heavily in Beecher's various projects and was known to purchase expensive clothing for his mentor. Through Beecher, Sage came to know his three crusading sisters: the author Harriet, and Catharine and Isabella, who were both actively working to improve the status of women. When Sage endowed a professorship at Yale, he named it to honor the Reverend Lyman Beecher, the father of this tumultuous clan of Christian reformers.

The poverty and humiliation experienced by his family during his youth had long-range influence upon Henry Sage. For many years, he was driven not only by singular ambition but also by the pressure of being his family's sole support. The economic dependence of his mother and sisters was a central factor in developing Sage's sensitivity to the importance of education for women. His close relationship with these women and his appreciation of their natural ability were recorded in his diary: "Mother and sisters are the same—kind, loving, affectionate—little Caroline is all I could wish—I think she will fill more than an ordinary station." He resolved that, if he prospered, he would educate her to any extent she desired. Upon winning a bet with a friend that entitled him to three dollars worth of books, he selected *The Female Student* for his sister Lucy.[15] When his sisters later encountered domestic difficulties, Sage again provided financial support. The women in Henry Sage's immediate family, who were little noted in history, aroused his interest in the education of women, particularly as an assurance of financial independence.

Despite the fact that she was an educated woman herself, Susan Linn Sage, Henry's wife, was not the prime mover in encouraging the admission of women at Cornell. Quite the contrary! The daughter of one of Ithaca's leading citizens, she had studied at the Albany Female Academy. Following her marriage in 1840, Susan had two sons and as the family prospered, achieved the ideal state of Victorian womanhood. Within her elegant home, she performed the functions of devoted wife and mother and was a cultivated, gracious hostess. The exemplar of Christian piety, she engaged in appropriately womanly activities in the church and in charitable organizations. Learning that Henry intended to encourage the admission of women at Cornell, his wife commented, "You have meant to do women a great good but you have ignorantly done them an incalculable injury."[16] The reasons for her objections remain obscured by the passage of time. One can only speculate that Susan Sage feared that coeducation would prove destructive of woman's traditional functions and her natural sphere.

When the university opened in 1868, there were 412 male students, the largest entering class of any American college of the period; a few grim, unfinished buildings set in a cornfield of Ezra Cornell's hilltop farm; and no women students. The opening ceremonies were a festive occasion, with a large crowd of spectators coming from all over New York State. In contrast to the jubilance of their audience, Andrew D. White and Ezra Cornell looked wan and weak. They both showed the effects of recent illnesses and exhaustion, incurred from the strain of the preparations. Each man was determined to appear at this auspicious occasion and to define publicly his aspirations for the new university which they had struggled to establish. Both made clear in their remarks their commitment to an added dimension which they hoped to develop in the future.

Revitalizing the principles of the People's College, Cornell described his goal that the institution would offer not only liberal education but practical education as well. Of even greater significance, he said, "I believe that we have made the beginning of an institution which will prove highly beneficial to the poor young men and poor young women of our country." [17]

Like Cornell, Andrew D. White had long considered co-education an integral part of his educational plans. He was also sensitive to the reluctance, widespread among others, to the implementation of this idea. Consequently, he adopted a strategy of reasonable persuasion in his remarks:

As to the question of sex, I have little doubt that within a very few years the experiment desired will be tried in some of our largest universities. There are many reasons for expecting its success. It has succeeded not only in the common schools, but what is much more to the point in the normal schools, high schools, the academies of this State. It has succeeded so far in some of the leading lecture rooms of our leading colleges that it is very difficult to see why it should not succeed in all their lecture rooms, and, if the experiment succeeds as regards lectures, it is very difficult to see why it should not succeed as regards recitations. Speaking entirely for myself I would say that I am perfectly willing to undertake the experiment as soon as it shall be possible to do so. But no fair-minded man or woman can ask us to undertake it now. It is with the utmost difficulty that we are ready to receive young men. It has cost years of hard thought and labor to get ready to carry out the

first intentions of the national and state authorities which had reference to young men. I trust the time may soon come when we can
do more.[18]

At the close of the ceremonies, John McGraw went to
White and reported, "My old business partner, Henry Sage,
who sat next to me during the exercises this morning,
turned to me during your allusion to Mr. Cornell with tears
in his eyes, and said: 'John, we are scoundrels to stand
doing nothing while those men are killing themselves to establish this university.' " Later the same day, Sage called
upon White. The obvious physical distress of Cornell and
White during the ceremonies had touched him and roused
him to immediate, direct action. Sage told White, "I believe
you are right in regard to admitting women, but you are
evidently carrying as many innovations just now as public
opinion will bear; when you are ready to move in this matter, let me know."[19] This positive response from Henry
Sage to the suggested adoption of coeducation was certainly
encouraging.

Those who stood to gain the most from it, women, were
also supportive. Indirectly, by her presence during the for-
mative years of the university, Elizabeth Agassiz had already provided convincing proof that, contrary to general
opinion, women could excel as scholars and scientists. It
was said that the achievements of this remarkable individual had established the fact that "women are capable of attaining to as consummate a degree of knowledge and culture in the zoological sciences as any man in the country."[20]
Elizabeth's husband Louis, the distinguished naturalist,
had been consulted before the university opened concerning curriculum and faculty. Professor Agassiz had then
been persuaded by Andrew D. White to serve as one of the
first nonresident lecturers at Cornell. Agassiz's ability as a
teacher and a scientist, and his prestige, strengthened the
new university. Although she had little scientific training
herself, Elizabeth learned quickly as she took notes on her

husband's lectures. She became an important research associate for his publications and eventually published her own texts in marine biology. Accompanying her husband on his scientific expeditions, she recorded their observations; in 1867, she was listed as coauthor of their highly regarded book *A Journey to Brazil.*

Other women were direct and specific in their advocacy of coeducation. Emily Howland approached Ezra Cornell and openly urged him to hasten the admission of women.[21] Cornell received a letter from the astronomer Maria Mitchell, who was the first woman elected to the American Academy of Arts and Sciences and a professor at Vassar College. Mitchell wrote to express her conviction that, although Vassar was the best institution of its kind in the world, it was not providing the best education for women. She reported having asked the president of Harvard how soon women would be able to attend that institution; the conservative estimate he gave her was twenty years. Mitchell expressed her hope that Ezra Cornell would admit women promptly to his university.[22]

Susan Anthony and Elizabeth Stanton observed events in Ithaca with much interest and each arranged visits there. It was Anthony's lecture in 1869 which attracted the most public attention. The student newspaper reported that "Miss Anthony has a pleasing delivery and an eloquent flow of language—and from an experience of over twenty years is the master of her role. . . . Her remarks on equal education of the sexes were cogent and pointed." Susan Anthony and a colecturer, Sarah F. Norton, did make pointed remarks, predicting that the day Cornell University admitted women would be celebrated as sacredly as the Fourth of July or the birth of Christ. Anthony confronted her host: she called upon Ezra Cornell to explain why women were still denied admission to the university. Cornell replied that any woman able to pass the competitive examinations for a state scholarship was qualified for admission. In order to assist low income students, the university charter had provided for one grant of free tuition in each Assembly district, the recipient to be determined by competitive examination. Ezra Cornell stated that if women had not entered, it was their fault, not his, thereby openly encouraging women to apply. Others were not yet so willing to admit women, believing the facilities and finances of the institution already taxed to the limit. In reporting Anthony's inflammatory speech, the student editor echoed words spoken on the opening day of the university, "Bid the daughters of the poor be patient, until the new enterprise is consolidated, the time propitious, and the way clear."[23]

Catharine Beecher, sister of Henry Ward Beecher and friend of Henry Sage, was a seasoned veteran of the campaign for female education and sought to impress her strong opinions on the founders of Cornell University.[24] A prolific writer and an effective lecturer, Beecher glorified women's domestic role, opposed woman suffrage and colleges like Vassar because they drew women outside the confines of the feminine sphere, and believed that education should train women for their sacred vocation within the home as wives, household managers, and mothers. At the same time, she anticipated the need for women to become trained teachers for the nation's children. Teaching was a vocation appropriate for women, she thought, and in addition would enable unmarried women to support themselves. There was a surplus of women in the country, Beecher noted, who were unable to find husbands because so many men had migrated west or had died in wars and shipwrecks.

Another function of female education that she advocated was the improvement of female health. Frequently in poor health herself, Beecher had conducted a survey of women acquaintances all over the country concerning their physical condition. These women reported frequent headaches, chills, tuberculosis, nervous disorders, and chronic invalidism. Convinced that American women were in an alarming

state of physical deterioration, she became one of the original advocates of physical education for women and counseled that most physical problems could be alleviated by
proper exercise, healthful diet, adequate ventilation, and
improved interior lighting.

In 1868, she addressed the New York State Teachers' Convention in Ithaca and Ezra Cornell observed, "I like Miss
Beecher pretty well but I must confess I like younger
women better. . . . She has ideas on reforming her sex, but
they are of the half bushel order."[25] Later, Beecher moved
to Ithaca, determined to take a course at Cornell although
Andrew D. White had cautioned her that no courses or
housing facilities were open to women. Cascadilla Place,
originally intended for Ezra Cornell's sanitarium, had been
converted into a dormitory for faculty and male students.
Declaring that she could live quite happily in this building
with men young enough to be her grandsons, she took the
course.[26]

Actually, Beecher opposed coeducation and suggested
that it would be advisable to educate women in an adjacent
institution designed for their particular needs and where
they could devote part of each day to domestic work. She
was eager to involve Mary White and Susan Sage in her
campaign as she believed there were many issues involved
which could only be discussed with mothers. Coeducation
posed many dangers, Beecher wrote to them, and unless
properly managed, would be like "bringing gunpowder and
burning coals into close vicinity." She knew that pure, good
women like themselves had little conception of the evils
that might befall sheltered, innocent girls.[27] Beecher's stern
views on the dangers implicit in coeducation had doubtless
been inflamed by attacks made upon her at this time by
Victoria Woodhull, the most radical of the feminists, who
persisted in linking women's rights with her own incendi-
ary opinions on free love.

In the early years of Cornell University's history, opinions on the shape of its future as an institution were many

and diverse. It is apparent from this background, however, that coeducation at Cornell exists not by accident but as the outgrowth of libertarian reform movements, the commitment of enlightened men, and the militancy of strong-minded women.

3 Sage College: Woman's Place at Cornell

> But however many other halls may be built, Sage College will always be most important, not only because this was the first, but because this magnificent gift of Henry Sage secured the rights and privileges of Cornell University for women students forever.
>
> Anna Botsford Comstock
> *A Half Century at Cornell, 1880–1930*

Despite the progressive intentions of the founders, there were still no women students at Cornell University two years after it opened. By 1870, however, there had been progress for women at other institutions. It was estimated that 3,000 women were studying in institutions awarding bachelor's degrees; of these, about 2,200 were in women's colleges, and only 800 attended coeducational institutions.[1] The concept of coeducation was adopted by most educators slowly, cautiously, and often reluctantly.

For example, the charter of the University of Michigan, the largest institution in the country, had provided for the admission of all qualified persons as early as 1837, but no funds were ever appropriated for women. In 1855, discussion of the issue of the admission of women surfaced at a state teachers' convention. In 1858 and 1859, several young women submitted their applications for admission but these were rejected. Women continued to demand entry to the university and pressure for enforcement of the charter was directed at the Board of Regents. These efforts were unavailing until February 1870 when the first woman student was finally accepted for admission.

At the same time, the University of Missouri granted admission to women in the Normal Department, a concession to the demand for teachers. When the women of Missouri had caused no trouble in this department, they were permitted to attend all lectures and recitations with men, provided they marched to class together in an orderly column guarded by teachers. When no problems were encountered within these limits, the women students were finally permitted to pray with the men in the university chapel.

At Cornell, the delay in admitting women was due primarily to the university's immediate success in attracting students. There were more men enrolled than could reasonably be accommodated in the few buildings available.[2] Students and faculty were housed together in the barracks-like confines of Cascadilla Place, which also was used for lectures and social events. White described it as "an ill-ventilated, ill-smelling, uncomfortable, ill-looking almshouse."[3] When Susan Anthony toured the building, she objected violently to the strong odor of tobacco and thought the place was badly in need of women.[4] Other students resided in the poorly heated and ventilated classroom-dormitories, White Hall and Morrill Hall. Plumbing was primitive and baths nonexistent.

Between the university and the town there was an expanse of a mile, an elevation of over four hundred feet, and fields, gullies, and rough paths which were alternately dusty, muddy, or buried in snow. Since some students boarded in town, and the overcrowded facilities at the university made it necessary to hold lectures in the Cornell Library downtown, there was continual hazardous travel uphill and down for both faculty and students, who often suffered undignified tumbles as they climbed back and forth.[5]

Despite these difficulties, the excellence of the faculty lectures made the hillside journey worthwhile. One of the stellar attractions was Professor Goldwin Smith.[6] A distinguished historian and professor at Oxford University, Smith belonged to the small group of British liberals, allied with John Stuart Mill, who were working for social reform.

Between 1868 and 1871, Cornell University did not appear to have facilities conducive to implementing the coeducational plan of its founders. In the overgrow[n] fields of Ezra Cornell's hilltop farm, only two utilitarian structures had been completed. Morrill Hall (*left*) and White Hall were already overcrowded with ma[le] students. (Cornell University, DMUA.)

On a lecture tour of the United States in 1864, Smith had been greatly impressed by the liberal views of Americans. When Cornell's president visited England, he was able to entice the cultured Oxford professor to join the radical educational experiment on the barren hilltop in central New York. Smith, anxious for a change of scene and a fresh challenge, agreed to serve as a lecturer in English and Constitutional History, with the understanding that he would accept no salary and could set his own schedule. Once settled in Ithaca, he was delighted with his new surroundings. The liberality of White, the character and generosity of Ezra Cornell, the faculty, the roughhewn students eager to learn, and the rugged beauty of the countryside excited him and involved him totally in this bold new venture. Goldwin Smith came to love Cornell University, he contributed his own books to the university library, he arranged for stonecarvers to come from England to decorate the new buildings, and he imported ivy from Oxford to beautify bare walls. Wearying of the communal life in Cascadilla Place, he made plans in 1870 to build his own cottage on the campus and hoped that in the event of his death and cremation, that wind would waft a few of his ashes to the campus at Cornell.[7]

But Smith grew increasingly troubled. Arriving in Ithaca in 1868, he was horrified to hear talk of the possible admission of women to the university; no one had mentioned such a possibility to him previously. After four months at Cornell, he wrote to a friend that he had been occupied fighting off the admission of women, an idea he characterized as "a crochet of Horace Greeley's."[8] In 1869, he addressed the social science convention in Albany, stating his view that everything affecting the relationship between the sexes was of utmost gravity. He believed that any experimenting should be made cautiously, on a very limited scale, and clearly stated his opposition to subjecting women to the rigors of competitive examinations.[9] Smith held earnest conversations with White and expressed his concern that any such efforts might make women unmarriageable.[10]

Delay on the question of coeducation was no longer possible in September 1870. The arrival of young Jennie Spencer from Cortland forced the issue. Spencer had passed the examination for a state scholarship and was therefore entitled to admission. She also carried a letter from a Cortland County official to Andrew White, which testified to her "irreproachable character." In view of the fact that her position as a woman student would be "a novel one," the men of Cortland County hoped that White would give Jennie Spencer every consideration.[11]

Housing for this lone female presented a problem. There were women residing in Cascadilla Place but they were wives of faculty members. This possibility was unthinkable for an unmarried young woman. So Spencer found a room in Ithaca and joined the hillside parade, struggling up and down several times a day in long skirt and petticoats. As the winter months wore on, she was exhausted by her hillside travel. Reluctantly, Jennie Spencer left Cornell, defeated by the lack of adequate housing for women on the campus.

Her failure to remain dramatized the practical aspect of instituting coeducation and alerted Henry Sage to the real needs of women at the university. Sage wrote to White in June 1871 that he would soon be coming to Ithaca and wished to discuss "a place for the education of women, under the wing of Cornell." [12] White had assumed that Sage might endow a professorship or a scholarship and was elated to learn that he wanted to contribute a building for women. [13] Jennie Spencer's struggles had not been in vain.

When the Board of Trustees met later that month, the announcement of Spencer's departure made a fitting preliminary for presenting Henry Sage's proposal to contribute funds for a women's building on the campus. In contrast to the admission of women to the University of Michigan or Missouri, which required long efforts to secure, their admission to Cornell was made comparatively easy by their benefactor, Henry Sage.

But Goldwin Smith and other influential faculty members, and some trustees as well, had already expressed their opposition to the admission of women. Students also had been very vocal in their antagonism to this idea. One of them wrote in the *Cornell Era:*

Almost universal experience has taught that though perfect order and serenity may prevail, ladies who are thus educated through the whole four years of a college course either spend the period in having "lovely" times with the young gentlemen, thus often destroying the advantages of both for completing the course, or come out those "strong bodied women with the strong minded views" of the Elizabeth Cady Stanton notoriety. And we fear that cases like the latter predominate largely. [14]

Consequently, White, a known advocate of coeducation, proposed that a study be made by the Board of Trustees to evaluate the effect of this new system upon women, men, and institutions. A committee of trustees was organized, with White and Sage designated to visit coeducational institutions. Although the investigation was to be thorough, the naming of these particular observers suggests that objectivity was not a prime concern. White, always a diplomatic strategist, appears to have been quite determined that the Sage proposal would be approved.

But the impatient women would wait no longer. In September, a few began to attend classes with the understanding that they could obtain degrees. This group included Emma Sheffield Eastman, a transfer student from Vassar College, who became in 1873 the first woman to graduate from Cornell University.

During the winter of 1871, White and his committee began gathering information on the merits and disadvantages of coeducation. After extensive correspondence with educators and reviews of reports prepared by other colleges and universities, White and Sage set forth to see for themselves some of these coeducational institutions. Their findings were published in a remarkable report, composed by White and presented to the Board of Trustees in February 1872.[15]

The investigation had been initiated by study of the 1858 report of the University of Michigan's Board of Regents. This report was of interest, White wrote, because it contained the opinions of many distinguished male educators. These men were decidedly opposed to coeducation. They declared it "contrary to nature," "likely to produce confusion," "at variance with the ordinances of God," and "dangerous." They predicted that "young men would lose a proper sense of dignity of their own pursuits," "the delicacy of the female character would be destroyed," and that "a present and local popularity might be gained but at a fearful ultimate expense and the disapprobation of men of science and learning throughout the country." White completely discounted the validity of this report because, although the men were learned experts, none of them had actual experience in coeducational institutions. Likewise, he discounted the many theories that had already been pro-pounded about woman, her intellectual capacity, and her proper sphere. The men of Cornell were determined to consider only evidence based on actual experience.

One example White presented to reassure skeptics and opponents was that coeducation had been going on in the academies and normal schools in New York and in neighboring states for almost a century. Letters from presidents of several normal schools were included in the report, which stated that their long experience with coeducation had been most satisfactory; the system had worked so well that it was now regarded as natural and normal, and "no evil" had been experienced. In fact, success had been achieved without proctors to restrain the young men or matrons to guard the young women.

White then offered the facts obtained from the tour he had made with Sage. First, they had visited Oberlin College where they dined in the college hall with two hundred students, evenly divided as to sex: "The order was excellent—the appearance of all neat and cleanly. The young men and women sat at the same table, on opposite sides; the conversation was quiet; there was, throughout, an air of refinement which the member of the Committee more familiar with college life has never seen at a table frequented by men alone." The order preserved impressed the visitors: "The Oberlin College table is probably the only one on the continent of which this can be said."

Order was also found to prevail in the classroom when the visitors observed recitations in mathematics and languages: "The young ladies, while showing self-possession, appeared refined, quiet and modest. Their exercises were in all cases performed as well as those of the young men, in many cases better." During their visit, a professor told White and Sage that in his long experience, he had found no difference between the sexes in their ability to perform in recitations. He took care to add that this experience did not prove conclusively that "there are not great differences in mental and moral characteristics between man and woman, fatal to the theories of those known as 'strong-minded women,' " but he could not recall a single instance of a "strong-minded" woman resulting from the system at Oberlin.

At Oberlin, the males were housed in dormitories. Females lived in a large, well furnished building supervised by a matron, who was assisted by a committee composed of faculty wives. Some students resided with local families, in which cases the females reported to the woman of the household, who was considered responsible for their conduct.

Opportunities for social contact between young women and men were regulated by the dictates of common sense. It had been found extremely conducive to the preservation of proper relations between the two sexes to have brothers and sisters attending Oberlin together since they were "mutually sensitive as to any thing that would tend to degrade each other." Coeducation had proven a great asset to the social life of the male student since he did not need "to make any expenditure of time, going out of his way or leaving his proper work, for the pleasure and improvement of society." Thus he was spared "the excessive introversion, the morbid fancies, the moroseness which sometimes arise in secluded study." Furthermore, it did appear that coeducation promoted not only order but also morality: "Evils that might be tolerated in the shape of drinking saloons and other places of dissipation, if young men only were present, seem intolerable when ladies are gathered with them."

In regard to the health and social development of young women, statistical studies had been conducted. One of them demonstrated that the death rate of Oberlin's women was quite similar to that of the men, despite the lower average life expectancy for women indicated in life insurance tables. Another showed that of the eighty-four graduates of the college course, only twenty-seven women remained unmarried.

The observations made by White and Sage at the University of Michigan were also included in the report. In contrast to Oberlin, no special building had been set aside for women. They were free to live where they pleased and to regulate their own activities. Men and women attended all classes together, except in the Medical College where classes were segregated by sex.

The facts at Michigan supporting the admission of women were impressive. The leading mathematician, who won a prize for the solution of a problem that had been unsolved for years, was a woman. One of the best Greek scholars was a woman. Statistics had been compiled pertaining to student performance in classical and scientific studies and by every measure, the women students had excelled. The women of Michigan were found to be not only dignified, modest, and refined, but also quite healthy. Socially, few problems had arisen from the mingling of the two sexes in a university town. The men seemed to be more interested in the daughters of the town's citizens than in their classmates: the women students "seem to be quietly on their guard against receiving too much attention from students of the other sex." The visitors even received a report from a janitor, who assured them that the presence of women had caused a great improvement in conduct in the hallways. The conclusions based on the Michigan visit were all very favorable, but White felt compelled to add one more important fact: "The general testimony was that the young lady students were more conscientious in study than the young men, and that this was the main cause of their remarkable success in every class and study."

Inspections by the two men at Northwestern University, at Illinois Industrial University (now the University of Illinois), and at Antioch College elicited further favorable testimony. The president of Antioch, the Reverend G. W. Hosmer, reported that, unlike the women at the University of Michigan, Antioch women were restricted to housing segregated by sex; and he firmly believed that, if coeducation were to succeed, "there must be separate halls for the young men and young women, and judicial regulations, and a parental watchfulness." Coeducation had greatly benefited the development of intellect and character of both men and women, he had observed, the young men becoming "more orderly, gentle, and manly," and the women "stronger and more earnest." Hosmer was convinced that better, more thorough education for women was vital to the welfare of society and that this goal could best be achieved through coeducation.

Having assembled numerous facts as a result of these investigations, White then developed some conclusions. First, he reported that all the evidence proved that the admission of women had a refining effect upon young men. Certainly, he thought it was a decided advantage for young men to associate with young women "whose thoughts and pursuits are of an ennobling kind." White was sure that college women would be of this type, speculating that "no frivolous young woman, no mere petted and spoiled beauty of a season, will be likely to wish to undergo the moral restraint or mental labor demanded in such a course, and if one were to enter from caprice, she would be certain to depart soon."

Second, the concern that association with young women might cause men to become effeminate was dispelled with the argument that coeducation would enhance their distinctly manly characteristics. To prove his point, White stated that "from no colleges did a more hardy, manly, brave body of young men go into our armies than from Oberlin and Antioch."

White next considered a prevalent concern that the presence of women would divert the men from their studies by arousing thoughts "more powerful than the love of learning." The conclusion was that men would study harder to appear to best advantage before the women and the conscientiousness of women would raise the level of scholarship.

Another subject of White's attention was the effect of coeducation upon young women, particularly their health. He referred to the studies of Dr. Edward Clarke, a respected professor at the Harvard Medical School, who was convinced that young women between the ages of fourteen and twenty were particularly susceptible to the strain induced by overexcitement, physical exercise, or "brain work." Such strain, Clarke said, when caused by coeducation, would induce neuralgia, uterine disease, and hysteria and might cause such imbalance in the system that children would be born deformed. White countered Clarke's frightening facts with his own observation. The college women White had seen on his trip were obviously as healthy as other women. He acknowledged that the deterioration of the health of American women was a very serious problem, but since there were so few women studying in colleges and so many unhealthy women, he did not believe that higher education could be considered the cause of it. The failure of men to find solutions to female health problems indicated clearly the need for educated women to address these issues. Furthermore, White asserted that college women must study physiology and hygiene, and any college building for women should be planned with special care in regard to the health of its occupants, with abundant light, adequate ventilation, and provisions for exercise.

Concluding from his own observations and those of others that coeducation would greatly enhance the development of feminine character and manners, White then discussed a very basic question. Since woman's sphere was different from that of man, did she require a different sort of education? An analogy was drawn between the physiological and intellectual needs of men and women: "As the bodies of men and women are built up by the same food, whether vegetable or animal, so it would seem that their minds and hearts and souls are to be built and beautified by the same moral, mental and aesthetical food." One could not assume from this argument, White thought, that the same education would encourage women to "any usurpation of unnatural functions, social or political." Instead, by fully developing her heart, mind, and soul, woman would be led to take her proper place and to fulfill even better the role which God intended for her, but "even if the most restrictive theory of woman's duties be accepted,—even if it be allowed that her only duties are those of a well-ordered household,—would she not be fitted better for her duties as the mother of future generations of citizens by courses of study large and broad, than by the unutterable inane instructions of the great majority of our ladies' boarding and 'finishing' schools?" He later cited Harriet Taylor Mill as an outstanding example of an educated woman who had ably managed her household and also had been intellectually productive.

Responding to fears that coeducational friendships might lead to marriage. White stated his belief that friendships formed in a university, based on thorough knowledge and similar interests, would be more desirable and stable than those which usually developed "by mere casual meeting, by an acquaintance of a few weeks, by winning manners at a ball" or "by a pleasing costume in the street."

As to the effect of the admission of women on Cornell University, White attempted to quiet the general fear that women students would lower the standards of scholarship. Women would take the same entrance examinations and be required to pass all other examinations to which men were subjected. In addition, all evidence pointed to the fact that women students did as well academically as men and sometimes better. White cited the example of Cornell's first woman student, Jennie Spencer, who had won a state scholarship and had also presented one of the best entrance examinations in 1870.

In case all the previous statements supporting coeducation failed to impress the trustees, White concluded his report with one final argument. Cornell University could not refuse much longer to try the coeducational experiment since it was, in a sense, a state institution and its charter specifically provided for the admission of "persons," the same persons who were studying in the public schools and academies of the state, "persons of both sexes."

White's advocacy of coeducation was reinforced by the official announcement that Henry Sage was willing to give Cornell University $250,000 on the condition that "instruction shall be afforded to young women . . . as broad and as thorough as that now afforded to young men." [16]

It is not surprising that the Board of Trustees voted to approve the report: as White later claimed, he intentionally exhausted all opposition by reading aloud the entire ninety pages. [17] The decision was therefore made that women would be admitted to Cornell University beginning in April 1872, approximately four years after the official opening of the institution. Originally women were required to be eighteen years old, but this provision was later abandoned.

Included in the White report were two different plans for the construction of accommodations for women, prepared during the previous winter by White, Sage, and the university architect. One proposal specified a central building with classrooms, surrounded by houses which could be rented to faculty families and also provide a homelike residence for women students. The other plan suggested one large building, incorporating lecture rooms, dormitory space, an infirmary, and a gymnasium.

Classrooms appeared in both proposals, since White, anxious to expand the study of science, had diplomatically convinced Sage that botany and horticulture were particularly appropriate studies for women. In this connection, work in the anticipated gardens would provide both fresh air and exercise to promote good health and also might help poor students earn money. Since Mary Ann Cornell's "system of industry" had not materialized, it was now suggested that Cornell women could increase their income by selling flowers grown in their own garden. The classrooms would in addition allow women to study physiology, a subject which propriety required be pursued separately from men.

Extensive consideration had already been given to the question of proper housing for women. Vice President William C. Russel wrote to White, expressing his opposition to the suggestion that individual houses rented to faculty families could also provide residential facilities suitable for women students. He urged White to put himself in the place of parents of these students:

Is every professor the right sort of man and every professorin the right sort of woman with whom to place young women? As good a person as the lady superintendent of Sage College would be? Who of them will undertake to prevent the evening appointments and country excursions so demoralizing to both parties? You will say, let the girls take care of themselves. I say not a day after we can take care of them as we would wish our daughters to be taken care of.[18]

The issue of supervision apparently did not influence White's decision. Ever the optimistic reformer, he believed in the innate goodness of humanity and in the ability of women as well as men to regulate their own lives. One can imagine his delight at the prospect of another reform effort, and his joy at having ample funds with which to construct a stately building that would add needed architectural strength and beauty to the campus. The single building plan was adopted.

The decision to admit women aroused mixed reactions. Vice President Russel was ecstatic. This was "one of the great triumphs of reason and conscience over prejudice which ought to be proclaimed in paeans from one end of the union to the other," he wrote to White. He considered the university a far more interesting institution than it had been previously because of this decision: "A light has fallen on it and it seems more human and refined and true than it ever did before."[19]

White's report and the decision to admit women also

brought favorable comment from those most affected. In a letter to White, a Connecticut woman wrote: "If you were a woman and had been disgusted, mortified and exasperated as I have been by the talk of educated men about our capacity, or incapacity rather, and what had better be done with us; I might make you understand the satisfaction, gratitude and delight with which I read your report. As it is you can never know anything about it. Please, can I have another copy?"[20]

A male student was less convinced about the wisdom of this decision and gazed balefully into the future: "Yes, we are to reform, we are to become scholarly past all record. There will be no more sprees and nocturnal carousals. Cards and billiards are to be a reproach. The filthy weed and flowing bowl are to be forsaken, because she is gazing on us. Terrible thought!"[21]

An even more unfavorable response to the admission of women was expressed by Professor Goldwin Smith. Smith abandoned his plans to construct a cottage on the campus, began to travel more extensively after 1870, and resigned in 1871. Several factors influenced this decision, among them the harshness of the Ithaca climate, Smith's poor health, his sense of intellectual isolation, and the increasing political tensions between the United States and Great Britain; but it was the issue of the admission of women that was decisive.[22]

Originally, Smith had endorsed John Stuart Mill's liberal effort to extend the franchise to women in England. He later denounced this reform effort and publicly repented his support of such a measure. Goldwin Smith declared himself an uncompromising opponent of female suffrage and explained that his previous endorsement was due to the fact that "he had not yet seen the public life of women in the United States."[23] American women, he had observed, had violated every tradition and law of nature: they had strayed beyond the proper feminine sphere to enter male professions, adopted male clothing, were now found in the sacred male sanctum of the smoking room, and had even taken up bicycle riding. In his view, women in the United States had broken all traditional bonds and were rapidly becoming unmanageable. Smith believed theoretically in the equality of the sexes, but he was adamant in his conviction that men and women had different abilities and roles in society, clearly differentiated by nature, and these differences necessitated special educational programs for each sex. Following this line of thought, he was convinced that women did not belong in the male community of university scholars. In addition, despite his usual alliance with liberal causes, Smith was opposed to the involvement of a new, struggling university in "every new hobby" before its reputation was established: "A University which, in advance of public opinion, offers itself as the corpus vile for public experiments, will certainly forfeit public confidence." He told White that if women were admitted, Cornell University would "sink at once from the rank of a University to that of an Oberlin or a high school" and all their hopes "of future greatness" for the institution would be lost, at least in his view.[24]

Smith kept hoping that "some Power of Good" would intervene to forestall the admission of women, but he was disappointed. Although he returned to give annual lectures, affirmed that the great satisfaction of his life had been his participation in the early struggles of a great institution, and bequeathed to the university the major portion of his large estate, Goldwin Smith always stood firm in his conviction that he could never be "a professor in an Oberlin."[25]

Meanwhile, the proponents of coeducation had persisted with their plans and by May 1873 were able to hold a ceremony, significant because it marked the laying of the cornerstone for the Sage College for Women. In his remarks, Henry Sage proclaimed that the occasion denoted "a new era in the history of education."[26] Somewhat overstating the facts, he said, "This is the first University in this country, if not in the world, which has at the same time boldly recognized the rights of woman as well as man to all the education she will ask, and pledges itself to the policy and duty of maintaining equal facilities for both."

Deploring the lack of development of woman's intellectual powers, Sage directed attention to the cause, the laws of every civilized nation: "Man has used his power over her, to say the least, unwisely and ungenerously. She has been restricted by legislation in her rights of property, in her freedom of action, in her power to elevate herself." It was time, he said, that "these old heresies be done away with; that woman shall have all rights which justly belong to her as a human being." Sage echoed Catharine Beecher's concern for the increasing number of women in the population in proportion to men, a fact which resulted from war, shipwrecks, and hazardous male employment, and noted that many women would be forced by these circumstances to support themselves and their families: "To fit them for these trials and duties, the doors of opportunity must be opened wide. All women should have the liberty to learn what they can, and to do what they have the power to do." He stated his high expectations for the result of coeducation:

The efficient force of the human race will be multiplied in proportion as woman, by culture and education, is fitted for new and broader spheres of action . . . when she is completely emancipated from unjust legal shackles, when she is as free as man is to seek her own path in life, wherever led by necessity or duty, hope or ambition, when opportunity and aid for culture in any direction are hers, then may we expect to see woman enlarged, ennobled in every attribute, and our whole race, through her, receive impulsion to a higher level in all things great and good!

The cornerstone of the building was then secured by Susan Sage, who maintained her conservative view of this revolutionary endeavor and expressed her hope that from this goodly structure would come "true Christian womanhood."

In the cornerstone, a box was sealed which contained newspapers, university documents, and a letter addressed by Ezra Cornell to the "coming man and woman." Cornell said in his remarks that he had set forth in this letter his thoughts on the possible failure of the coeducational experiment, if it ever did fail, which he hoped it would not. Since no copy of the letter was made and the contents were not disclosed to anyone, Cornell's views remain a mystery, enclosed within the walls of Sage College. Ezra Cornell died in 1874. He never saw Sage College completed or the results of his farsighted plan to extend educational opportunity to women.

Other speakers joined in celebrating this auspicious occasion, among them Colonel Homer Sprague, a former Cornell professor who was at that time the principal of the Adelphi Academy in Brooklyn. Sprague said women needed higher education in order to be able to support themselves, if necessary, and he enumerated the occupations newly opened to women such as journalism, lecturing, preaching, medicine, and teaching, for which they must be able to prepare themselves. If, on the other hand, women remained within the home, he thought they needed higher education to forestall the temptations of "gossip, fashion-worship, pleasure-hunting, dissipation, and vice." Considering the possibility that a college education might deflect woman's attention from home and household affairs, Sprague pointed out that Elizabeth Browning's intellectual achievements did not make her any less admirable as wife and mother. He considered Emma Willard the living illustration of Wordsworth's "perfect woman, nobly planned." Then he said: "After all, not matrimony but character, not widowhood nor motherhood, but moral and intellectual strength and beauty is the great object of woman's existence. It is a common and most pernicious mistake to teach a girl that unwedded life is a failure. Happy she can be, with Milton, 'married to immortal verse,' or can say with Michael Angelo, 'I have espoused my lot; my works shall be my children.' "

One man would not have been expected to participate in

this event signalizing progress in the education of women, but he, too, appeared to grace the occasion with his remarks. Goldwin Smith paid tribute to the benevolence of Henry Sage, who was unselfishly using his wealth to benefit society. Smith proclaimed that, as an educator, he was vitally interested in improved education for women and had even participated in the formation of classes for women in Canada.[27] But he qualified his endorsement of coeducation by saying, "in removing artificial privileges and artificial barriers, let us take care that we do not attempt to remove the great land marks of nature, or encourage in the sexes the belief that they are rival competitors, instead of being helpmates." Ever gracious in his comments, Smith stated that since he had the greatest respect for Andrew White and the Cornell faculty, he was inclined to defer to their opinions in this matter, although he differed with them.

In reality, Smith's presence had nothing to do with the admission of women. He had abruptly canceled another engagement and rushed to Ithaca to stand with his friends at Cornell who were again the center of controversy.[28] Three days before, the charge had been made again on the floor of the legislature that Ezra Cornell had subverted the intent of the Morrill Act and was attempting, by treachery and fraud, to utilize the land grant funds to amass a fortune for himself. The return of Goldwin Smith was caused not by any change of opinion on the question of coeducation but rather by the fact that the man he so admired, Ezra Cornell, was the target of unjust, vicious accusations of wrongdoing. The Sage College ceremonies provided an incongruous but opportune public forum for Smith to reaffirm his faith in Ezra Cornell and Cornell University.

With the exception of Goldwin Smith's remarks, the ceremony and speeches at Sage College marked an auspicious beginning for this new venture in the education of women. The rhetoric of the day proposed a broader view of the potential of women than had previously been put forth in such specific terms. However, actual implementation proved frustrating. Because of delays and disputes, the first official occupants of Sage College did not move in until the fall of 1875. Henry Sage and his family were so delighted with the building that they had vacationed there the previous summer.

White and Sage devoted themselves single-mindedly to the planning and execution of this project. The care and attention they gave to every detail suggest that they were determined to entice women students into their coeducational enterprise rather than to meet a pressing social need, equal education for women. It is difficult now to envision the president of a university personally selecting items of furniture, correcting mistaken charges from manufacturers, and urging a carpet dealer to send up a competent rug man since the carpenter's measurements were not trustworthy, which is precisely what White did.[29]

While Sage wanted this building to be homelike, White wanted to construct an architectural masterpiece, the realization of his collegiate dreams. To this end, the stonecarvers from England were set to work to embellish the facade of the structure. For the interior, plans were made to surround the women with such objects of beauty and taste as engravings and sculpture from Berlin, Paris, and London.

Of even greater importance to White, Sage, and Catharine Beecher, Sage College contained every possible provision to ensure the good health of its inhabitants. In response to inquiries, a brochure was published which described the many benefits of this marvelous edifice, situated in the "high and healthful region in the midst of the beautiful scenery of the headwaters of Cayuga Lake."[30] Sage College was heated by steam, lighted by gas, and provided with water and all modern conveniences; baths on every floor, a gymnasium, a sheltered corridor for walking in bad weather, special air shafts, an abundance of windows for good ventilation, and excellent drainage. There were beau-

Sage College, as it appeared in the late 1800s, was an outstanding example of Victorian gothic architecture and a lasting symbol of the founders' aim to educate women along with men at Cornell. In this dormitory, designed to promote their intellectual, social, and physical development, generations of Cornell women were sheltered in splendor from 1875 until World War II. (Cornell University, DMUA)

tifully landscaped grounds and botanical gardens where "the ladies could have practical and healthful instruction." In addition to spacious public rooms for the use of the students, the private rooms were arranged for two women with specific areas for study and sleep. Henry Sage was particularly concerned about beds for females and for health reasons, wanted each young woman to have her own bed with high quality mattresses and springs. The trustees planned to provide an abundance of healthful, nourishing food. Also, there would be a thorough course of lectures on physiology and hygiene given each year, which all students would be required to attend. In case all these meticulous provisions failed, there would be an infirmary available, and in addition White ordered four easy chairs for invalids.[31]

While living in Sage College, women would have access to a nearby chapel, musical instruction which was taught "as a science and an art in a manner worthy of a University," and to lectures by such distinguished men as James Russell Lowell and Louis Agassiz.[32] They would also be able to use five laboratories, four drawing rooms, the university library, which was surpassed only by the facilities at Harvard and Yale, and the scientific collections maintained by the university. Cornell University, it was reported, was a particularly attractive place for women intending to be teachers since "no ladies' college in the land, no matter how excellent its arrangements may be, places at the disposal of lady students such attractions in instruction."

It was estimated that $325.00 would be sufficient to provide tuition ($75.00 per year), board at Sage College ($4.00 per week for forty weeks), room rent ($1.50 per week), laundry, and books. Provisions were made for a reduction in cost for young women "of excellent social standing" who lacked sufficient funds, and it was suggested that women could earn money by doing light work at Sage College or through private tutoring.

In the brochure, assurance was given that Sage College

was not intended for women who merely wanted to acquire a few accomplishments: "A university education is for young ladies who have a real taste for study and desire for knowledge: who aim to prepare themselves so that in case of adversity, they may be sure of a good self-support, and who have the fixity of purpose and definiteness of aim necessary to carry them through a thorough course of advanced study." If any question remained about the propriety of coeducation, it was pointed out that "the difference between a college where ladies are not admitted and one to which they are admitted is the difference simply between the smoking car and the car back of it, between the room where none but men are admitted and the room to which gentlemen and ladies are admitted on equal terms."

No crowding would be permitted in Sage College, which could accommodate only 120 women, so candidates for admission were urged to apply as soon as possible. But when Sage College opened in the fall of 1875, only twenty-nine women were in residence, a condition described as scarcely enough women "to keep the ghosts out of the corners."[33] Twenty other women students attended Cornell University but were living at home, with relatives, or in boarding houses. Although the founders of Cornell were genuinely anxious to include women in their educational experiment, apparently few others in 1875 were prepared to accept their thesis that women should have the same opportunity as men.

In the early years of coeducation, under the strong leadership of President White, opportunities for women were strikingly similar to those of the men at Cornell. Women were admitted on the basis of their proven ability and their performance on the entrance examination. In the competition for state scholarships, the rules stated that no distinction on the basis of sex would be permitted: the aim of the competition was to secure the best scholars for Cornell University.[34] The educational system at the time was largely unstructured, and there was wide variation in the preparation of entering students. Some like Anna Botsford Comstock and Susanna Phelps Gage came from village schools in the rural areas of the state while others like Florence M. Kelley and Ruth Putnam, from distinguished families in urban centers, had been educated at home or in private schools. Julia Thomas Irvine completed a bachelor's degree, begun at Antioch College, and then earned a master's degree. Because of her extensive education at a Quaker boarding school, eighteen-year-old Carey Thomas immediately qualified to study on the junior class level.[35] At Cornell, women were judged academically on the basis of their ability, not their gender.

Because Cornell University was a relatively new institution and an early advocate of the elective system, students had great freedom of choice in selecting curriculum. Susanna Gage was one of the first women to do laboratory work in physics. One of the first women to hold a state scholarship and to receive a degree, Sophy P. Fleming was qualified to obtain a Bachelor of Arts degree. Most women did not come well enough prepared in Latin, Greek, and mathematics to pursue this particular course of study. Kate Gleason, the first woman to study mechanical engineering, donned her overalls and worked in the engineering shops with the men.[36] An able woman with adequate preparation could enter the program of her choice.

Theoretically, Andrew D. White opposed the dormitory system because he feared the disciplinary problems and disorder observed at colleges for men, but the absence of adequate housing on the Ithaca hilltop compelled the university to provide residential facilities.[37] Housing was available for men in Cascadilla Place and for women in Sage College. Dormitory residence was not obligatory for either males or females and the university took no official responsibility for supervising or regulating the lives of either sex.

Women as well as men had the opportunity to study on the graduate level. In 1880, Cornell University awarded to May Preston a Ph.D. degree, the first such degree granted to a woman at this institution.[38] After serving as a professor of Greek and English, May Preston Slosson moved to Laramie, Wyoming, where she was appointed by the governor to serve as chaplain of the State Penitentiary for Men, reputedly one of the first women to hold such a position.

The highest level of education had been reached three years earlier by Helen Magill when she received a Ph.D. degree, the first awarded to a woman in the United States, from Boston University.[39] Her career as an educator eventually led to her meeting Andrew D. White, who was now a lonely widower. In 1890, they were married. When she was not abroad with her husband on diplomatic assignments, Helen White lived on the Cornell campus, where she took an active, personal interest in the women students.

The first Doctor of Science degree awarded to a woman in the United States was granted by Cornell University to Carolyn Baldwin Morrison in 1895.[40] As an undergraduate at the University of California, she had been the first woman to graduate from the Department of Mechanics and had been elected to Phi Beta Kappa. At Cornell, she was elected to Sigma Xi for the excellence of her work in physics. She later returned to California, where she taught physics and coauthored a physics textbook.

During this period, Cornell University promoted several other innovations in higher eduation for women. Certainly the initial emphasis that Ezra Cornell and Andrew White placed on providing access to higher education for those outside the economic elite and the provisions they made for state scholarships did benefit both women and men. In 1884, additional scholarships were made available from funds contributed by Henry Sage, with three scholarships to be awarded specifically to females based on competition in the annual entrance examinations. As a result, Cornell University became one of the earliest institutions to provide direct financial encouragement for able women, regardless of their social and economic status. In contrast, the women's colleges directed their efforts primarily to the daughters of wealthy professional men.[41]

Cornell University also developed a course in social work in 1885, one of the first in American higher education and the idea was rapidly adopted by the women's colleges as a field of study well suited to assumed female interests. Bryn Mawr College offered a course in Charities and Corrections in 1888, followed by Vassar College in 1894.[42]

Twenty years after the opening of Sage College, the alumnae prepared a report as a tribute to Henry Sage, who was now over eighty years old. A thorough study of the educational, social, and occupational development of Cornell alumnae had been compiled so that Sage could judge for himself whether his generous gift and his hopeful prophecies at the laying of the Sage College cornerstone had been fulfilled.[43]

The graduates reported that in 1895 Sage College was filled to capacity with 104 women in residence and a total of 224 enrolled in the university. Over the twenty years, 990 women had attended Cornell and 325 received degrees, fifty-five of which were graduate degrees. That only one-third of the women students had obtained degrees they attributed to the fact that many of the nongraduate women were teachers seeking specialized training, although a college degree was not yet required for their work.

In this report, the initial fears of the disastrous effect of coeducation upon women were conclusively refuted. Seventy-six percent of the women surveyed reported they were in good health. Some considered themselves in better health after college than they had been at entrance, and only seven percent thought themselves less healthy after college. Evidence of their physical fitness was the fact that only eight women were known to have died, from causes totally unrelated to their education, and only one of these had died in childbirth. Fifty percent of the women were married, a low proportion in relation to the total population, but understandable because many women were older than average when they came to Cornell. It was thought that they had already made a conscious decision not to marry and preferred to pursue a career. In addition, coeducation had not appeared to diminish woman's effectiveness as mother but rather, the women believed, had made them better mothers. Many reported, however, that their ignorance about their own bodies and those of their children had been a definite handicap. Through a study of academic records, it was determined that women had not lowered the academic standards but had excelled scholastically; a higher proportion of women than men had done outstanding work. More women held undergraduate scholarships in proportion to their numbers than men and had done equally as well qualifying for graduate fellowships. Women were a small proportion of the total enrollment, but they had won consistently more than their share of honors. Half of the most recently elected members of Phi Beta Kappa were women.

This tribute by the alumnae to Henry Sage ended appropriately with an account of the achievements of some graduates. Cornell women had excellent academic preparation for professional service as teachers and administrators throughout the educational system. Seventeen recent graduates were studying toward advanced degrees at American and foreign universities, and several were among the first women students to gain admission to these institutions. Others had entered professions previously reserved for men, such as medicine, scientific research, business, and social service. In conclusion, the alumnae found that education in a great university did for women precisely what it did for men. It promoted intellectual growth, the full development of natural abilities, and often, the mastery of specialized skills. Whether women fulfilled their traditional roles within the home or were active participants in the nondomestic world, they were able to function with intelligence and competence because they had a Cornell education.

In an account of the early years of university history, it is important to consider the achievements of a few women who did respond to the promise of equal education at Cornell. Carey Thomas, denied admission to Johns Hopkins Graduate School because of her sex, went abroad to study and became the first foreigner and woman to win a Ph.D. at the University of Zurich, the only European institution admitting women at the time. In addition to her position as president of Bryn Mawr College, she later assumed active leadership in the suffrage movement. Julia Thomas Irvine became a professor of Greek at Wellesley College, and in 1895 was elected the fourth president of Wellesley. Florence Kelley, at the suggestion of Carey Thomas, studied at the University of Zurich, developed her interest in social reform, and later became an active participant with Jane Addams at Hull House. Her studies of labor conditions in Illinois led to the early introduction of protective legislation for women and children in that state and to her appointment as Chief Factory Inspector for the state. A formidable crusader, Kelley devoted her life to the improvement of working conditions for women and children through legislation and through her leadership of the National Consumers' League. Susanna Gage collaborated with her husband in zoological research and became a highly regarded embryologist in her own right. She was technically unemployed but her research was of such high quality that she, along with her husband, was selected for listing in *American Men of Science*. She was one of the very few women designated in this volume as an eminent scientist in the estimation of her colleagues. Anna Botsford Comstock gained early acclaim as an engraver and illustrated her husband's texts in entomology. Later she became involved in the nature study movement; her research, lectures, and textbooks lifted the study of nature to the level of an academic subject in schools and colleges across the nation. Kate Gleason achieved her greatest distinction as the business promoter of the gear-cutting machinery manufactured by her family in Rochester, as a pioneer in suburban development with low-cost standardized housing units, the first woman member of the American Society of Mechanical Engineers, and the first woman president of a bank. As the result of her research and publications, Ruth Putnam was for many years the principal American scholar on the history of the Netherlands.[44]

History has proven that the faith which Ezra Cornell, Andrew D. White, and Henry Sage had in women was well justified. When the League of Women Voters elected twelve outstanding living American women in 1923, three of these women were Cornellians: M. Carey Thomas, Anna Comstock, and Martha Van Rensselaer, the founder of the home economics program at Cornell.[45]

The appeal of coeducation continued to attract women as the years passed, and the facilities of Sage College were soon inadequate to meet the demand for housing for women. Andrew D. White, although no longer president of the university, maintained an active interest in its development, and in 1910 he undertook a personal campaign to secure additional dormitory facilities for women.

He carried on extensive correspondence with Mrs. Russell Sage, a former acquaintance from Syracuse and an individual known to be interested in women's education.[46] Mrs. Sage had been dispensing large sums of money from her husband's estate to charitable and educational institutions since his death in 1906. She intended through these gifts to benefit society, to memorialize the Sage family and, most of all, to redeem her late husband's reputation—he had not been noted during his lifetime for his social concern nor his generosity. In response to her letter expressing interest in the education of women at Cornell, White replied to describe for Olivia Sage the achievements of women, their scholastic success, their social usefulness as mothers and in charitable, religious, and educational work. He wrote about the equality that women enjoyed at Cornell and said that their presence in the university had promoted "decency and

Florence Kelley '82 committed her life to social reform. She fought for wage and hour laws for women workers, opposed child labor, and made many proposals later implemented in federal legislation. Of this dynamic woman, it was said that "everybody was brave from the moment she walked into the room." Kelley was also a founder of the NAACP and the Women's International League for Peace and Freedom. (Underwood & Underwood.)

Anna Botsford Comstock '85 shown here as an undergraduate student, was, in 1888, one of the first four women elected to Sigma Xi, the national honorary society for scientific achievement founded at Cornell University. A pioneer in the field of nature study education, she wrote the *Handbook of Nature Study*, (1911), a text so popular that it has appeared in twenty-four editions and eight languages. Her marriage to John Henry Comstock was notable for their sharing of professional interests as well as domestic chores. (Cornell University, DMUA.)

Margaret Floy Washburn Ph.D '94 was one of the first graduate students to study at Cornell with the eminent psychologist, E. B Titchener. From 1900 to 1902 she served as Warden of Sage College and taught psychology classes. A professor of psychology at Vassar College, Washburn's teaching, research, and professional leadership led ultimately to her election in 1931 as a member of the National Academy of Sciences, the second woman to be so honored (Courtesy of the National Academy of Sciences.)

Gail Laughlin LL.B. '98 was forceful advocate of equal rights for women. In 1919 she was founder and first president of the National Federation of Business and Professional Women's Clubs Determined to promote legal equality for women, Laughlin campaigned for woman suffrage and was one of the first women elected to the Maine legislature. leader of the National Woman Party, she urged passage of the Equal Rights Amendment. (Courtesy of the National Federation of Business and Professional Women's Clubs.)

Nora Stanton Blatch '05 carried on the crusade for women's rights initiated by her grandmother, Elizabeth Cady Stanton. She is shown here in 1913 astride a horse, urging a male audience to support woman suffrage. The first woman to earn a degree in civil engineering at Cornell, Blatch was selected in 1943 by the General Federation of Women's Clubs as one of the two outstanding women in the engineering profession. (United Press International photo.)

order." This last point proved to be the most convincing, for Mrs. Sage was also deeply interested in the cause of woman suffrage. She became hopeful that women might have as salutary an effect in politics as they did in the lecture rooms of Cornell University. In 1911, this leading female philanthropist agreed to contribute $300,000 to construct a second residence for women, to be named Prudence Risley Hall in honor of her husband's mother.

White's persuasive arguments were effective and he is generally credited with obtaining some of the Sage bounty for Cornell.[47] The primary motivation for this gift, however, can be traced to an earlier time and to Olivia Sage's friendship with Elizabeth Stanton, who had a long-standing interest in coeducation and Cornell University.[48] Sage and Stanton had become associated through their mutual interest in Emma Willard's Seminary from which both had graduated. Eventually, Stanton succeeded in converting the younger woman to the cause of woman suffrage. They often

Jessie Fauset '05 (*left*), shown with fellow writers Langston Hughes and Zora Hurston, was reputedly the first black member of Cornell's Phi Beta Kappa chapter. She was a teacher as well as a novelist, a poet, and literary editor of the *Crisis*, a publication of the NAACP. (Courtesy of the NAACP.)

Agnes Gouinlock Conable (*left*, on the steps of Sage College) and Jane Gouinlock VanArsdale, both members of the Class of 1908, applied their Cornell education as wives, mothers, and civic leaders. Each married and had three sons who graduated from Cornell. Each had one daughter-in-law who was a Cornellian and three grandchildren who attended Cornell. (Author's photograph.)

Martha Van Rensselaer '09 (*second from left*) traveled across New York State with other home economists to provide education for married women. She believed that woman's work was important and that it merited the attention of educators and scientists. With Flora Rose, she created the College of Home Economics and an extension program to train women to provide nutritious food, functional clothing, and a wholesome domestic environment. (Cornell University, DMUA.)

Georgia Harkness '12, an or
dained Methodist minister, foun
few professional opportunities f
women in the church b
achieved distinction as a teache
theologian, and author. Harkne
wrote numerous devotional
poems, and hymns, and mo
than thirty-six books, includir
Women in Church and Socie
(1972) in which she advocated
larger role for women in chure
leadership. In recognition of h
own career as a religious leade
she was honored by the Gener
Federation of Women's Clubs
1941 and was elected Churc
woman of the Year in 1958. (Cou
tesy of Abingdon Press.)

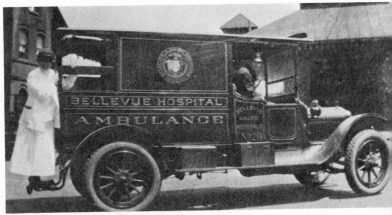

When Connie Guion received her degree in 1917 from the Cornell Medical C
lege, she was thirty-five years old. For over fifty years, she was a dedica
physician and inspiring teacher. Guion was the first woman in the United St
to serve as professor of clinical medicine. She directed the outpatient clinic at
New York Hospital–Cornell Medical Center, where the outpatient building r
bears her name. Guion encouraged other women to enter the field of medici
believing it was the most satisfying profession for those "who desire it intens
for the well-endowed, the strong and brave." (New York Hospital—Cornell M
cal Center, Medical Archives.)

discussed the importance of equal education for women and, specifically, the progress of women at Cornell.[49] In 1895, President Jacob Gould Schurman attempted to interest the wealthy Russell Sage in endowing a professorship in civil engineering at Cornell. Stanton's advice to Sage's wife was that any financial aid given to Cornell should benefit women students, as the men had always been well provided for by the university. Olivia Sage agreed with this view and so apparently did her husband, as he did not consent to Schurman's appeal. Elizabeth Stanton's suggestion of financial assistance to benefit the women of Cornell did not come to fruition for almost twenty years, following Stanton's death and that of Russell Sage, when Olivia Sage acted upon her friend's advice and agreed to endow a second elegant home for women at Cornell.

In the intervening years, several other dormitories have been constructed for women. Now Sage College no longer stands alone as a majestic edifice, surrounded by exotic gardens and expansive lawns. It is a quaint relic of an earlier period, hemmed in on all sides by modern buildings which house classrooms for engineers and hotel students, and offices for university administrators. The significance of Sage College remains an integral, vital part of the university heritage, however, for its construction made possible the admission of women and insured that they would always have a place at Cornell.

4 The Education of Womanly Women and Manly Men, 1885–1960

> I want to have girls educated in the university, as well as
> boys, so that they may have the same opportunity to be-
> come wise and useful to society that boys have.
>
> Ezra Cornell
> To Eunice Cornell, 1867

Sage College provided a suitably stately setting for social and cultural events in the early years at Cornell. Over
100 students, both female and male, gathered in the Botanical Lecture Room one winter evening to hear a poetry
reading by one of the university's most loved and most
colorful professors.[1] Hiram Corson, a somewhat eccentric
figure with a flowing beard, who fancied richly colored
vests and held unorthodox beliefs in the power of spiritualism, attempted to cultivate a love of literature among the
students through public readings, which he delivered with
dramatic verve.

Elizabeth Barrett Browning's work was the subject of Corson's enthusiastic presentation on this occasion. It was received with equal enthusiasm by the students, many of
whom had brought along their own copies in order to fully
appreciate his interpretation. Browning's sentiments ap-
pealed both to Corson and to the youthful liberals who were
students at Cornell in the early days. Some had organized
their own informal Browning groups to enjoy together her
humanitarian themes in such works as the one Corson
chose to read, a novel in verse entitled *Aurora Leigh*. In this
work, Browning suggests that every person, female or male,
is an independent individual solely responsible for personal
thoughts and actions. Her view contrasted sharply with the

popular concept which held that woman was destined to remain dependent upon man. Further, she described a new kind of relationship between women and men in this passage:

> The world waits
> For help. Beloved, let us work so well,
> Our work shall still be better for our love
> And still our love be sweeter for our work.

Browning's poetic vision of individual integrity and mutuality between the sexes reflected the aspirations of many nineteenth-century reformers: Susan B. Anthony carried a copy of this poem with her constantly as a source of encouragement.[2]

It was this same vision of equality which originally motivated Ezra Cornell and Andrew D. White to conceive their coeducational university, guided by the leading principle that every person was worthy of educational opportunity regardless of sex. Their commitment to this goal placed Cornell University in the vanguard of the movement for coeducation. Of all the educational institutions in the United States in 1870, only 29 percent were coeducational. That these men were leaders in a popular reform is proven by the fact that a century later, over 86 percent of all institutions had adopted this form.[3] It has been generally assumed that the educational experiences of women and men were equal because they were similar. In 1973, however, a major study of women in higher education, conducted by the Carnegie Commission on Higher Education, analyzed the actual implementation of coeducational goals, reporting wide variations in the degree of success and alleging that Cornell University had maintained restrictive policies in regard to women for many years.[4] It is imperative therefore to look beyond the early period of university history to measure the impact of the original promise of equity in education.

A crucial shift of university policy toward women took place after the high hopes of Andrew D. White and Henry

Sage for the success of Sage College had been disappointed. The building was not fully occupied for almost twenty years. Sage had worried from the beginning about the propriety of women residing in Sage College without supervision and had written to White expressing grave concern about this freedom and the potential of moral dangers.[5] When friendly interclass rivalry erupted into an unladylike scuffle in the stately halls of Sage, he was convinced that the women were in need of regulation. It was rumored that a chaperone would be installed in Sage College, a suggestion that the independent women found insulting to their integrity.[6] They aimed to demonstrate that they could take care of themselves by organizing a student government association and agreeing on rules of conduct and penalties for misbehavior.

By 1879, the entire university was in a precarious condition: enrollment had declined and costs were higher. The anticipated increase in number of women in Sage College had not materialized, and Andrew D. White became greatly concerned. He convened a meeting of Sage residents in April, proposing that more stringent rules be invoked and a matron engaged to provide a more orthodox environment. The women protested these proposals and were supported in their struggle for independence by the male editors of the *Era:*

Doubtless many anxious parents have kept their daughters away from Cornell, fearing some harm from the freedom here allowed. This action implies that their daughters need close restraint; if so, Cornell does not want them. If so, send your "Daisy Millers" elsewhere. The young women for whom the Sage endowment was given have too much purpose in being here, and are too womanly, to need the iron boardinghouse rules in regard to social intercourse with their gentlemen friends.[7]

White did not press the matter, instead he left to assume a diplomatic post as minister to Germany. The following fall, new rules of conduct, composed by Henry Sage, went into effect at Sage College.[8] The women continued to insist on their own ability to enforce these regulations, and the concept of a matron remained abhorrent to them.

Applications to live in Sage College did not increase, and Susan Sage was heard to remark that her husband's generosity in providing the new building had produced a failure.[9] White and Sage considered the possibility of renovating the dormitory into a site for a college of engineering and architecture, but did not take action.[10]

In 1883, Sage wrote to a friend complaining that "Cornell has not done justly toward me nor toward women, in the method of administering my gifts for the education of women." His contributions, he was convinced, entitled him to a strong voice in the management of Sage College. He wanted a system established that would protect young women and gain the support of their parents, and he began searching for a woman who could establish control over the residents of Sage.[11] The Board of Trustees ratified Sage's view and in 1884 ruled that henceforth all women would be required to live at Sage College. This new policy was printed in a brochure and mailed to all women students who had left the campus for vacations at home.[12]

After extolling the great generosity in providing for the comfort, health, and pleasure of the residents, the trustees stated that the building must be fully utilized or else given up by the women. If that happened, the most generous provisions made by any university for women would amount to nothing and students would be forced to find rooms at higher prices far from the campus "with no provision for comfort and enjoyment as at present, no general parlors, no baths, no special reading or society rooms, no pleasing surroundings," and still their housing would cost more. It was announced that a woman of high social position had been engaged to serve as lady principal and that the professor of physical culture would provide special gymnastic training for women.

If some women found the cost of living in Sage College beyond their means, it was suggested they could apply for financial assistance. The trustees did not want any woman to attempt to save fifty or sixty cents a week by depriving herself of the "well-ventilated rooms, good food, opportunities for exercise, bathing, and social improvement" available in Sage College. Such false economy they thought, would be harmful to the women students, the university's reputation, and to the nation. It would be far better for such women to forego a university education than to undermine their constitutions and go out from Cornell "as just one more addition to the great number of sickly, weakly, weary American women, unfit for any duty requiring bodily or intellectual vigor."

The cooperation of the women was strongly urged so that Sage College could become what it was intended to be—"a blessing to the whole body of lady students in attendance, and to the education of women throughout the world." Anyone who did not wish to comply could obtain an honorable dismissal and depart with the best wishes of the board, the founder of Sage College, and the faculty. The new requirement was put into effect in September 1884.

During this period, Ellen C. Brown '82, an aide in President White's personal library, took the liberty of expressing her opinions on this matter to her employer. She was convinced the new ruling would attract immature school girls "who will do the University little credit and the cause of coeducation much harm": it was an admission of failure of the system of equality between the sexes.[13] White replied that it was not any fault of the women but that the founder of Sage College had decided that his generous gift was not better utilized because parents "feel the need of such a Lady Directress to give tone and character to the place in the eyes of the public." Brown later issued a further objection:

We obstinately continue to see that by this action the Board of Trustees has for the first time made a distinction between the men and women of the University, exerting a control over the personal life of the women which it does not exert and would not think of exerting over the men. . . . When every step of progress and especially every step in which the position of women is concerned, is gained at such cost, we can not help noting with pain a backward step, a move toward putting woman back into the position she held when she was considered fit for no broader life than that for which the foundations were laid in the young ladies seminary.

Stella Spencer and Emma Bassett, also recent graduates, then joined forces with Ellen Brown to organize a more effective assault on the Board of Trustees and their ruling. Some discreet advice on the project was given by Professor Simon H. Gage and his wife, Susanna, although they believed the faculty should not become openly involved. The following June, fifty-two alumnae sent to the Board of Trustees, in identical printed form, their petition protesting the new regulation.

The women protested the use of compulsion in determining their place of residence and the making of arbitrary distinctions between the two classes of students, male and female. Since women students had already proven themselves quite competent to direct their own lives during the twelve years of coeducation at Cornell and since students had never before been denied personal liberty in order to utilize university property economically, the new law was deemed unnecessary and unwise. Statements had been solicited by the alumnae from the presidents of the University of Michigan, the University of Minnesota, the University of Wisconsin, and Oberlin College, all testifying to the wisdom of free choice in the selection of residence for both men and women students.

The petitioners further stated that "it seems that the chief function of a university is to promote the full and untrammeled development of each student in accordance with the law of his own nature." Citing the university's original Plan of Organization and its statement that "the great and leading principle is the absolute and essential importance of human development in its richest diversity," the women voiced their wholehearted support for this goal and protested that "compulsion in the matter of one's private life is directly opposed to the accomplishment of that purpose."

Letters from individual alumnae were included to bolster their argument. One woman wrote that having the freedom to select one's own living accommodations was far better preparation for later life than the artificial method of restricting women to special facilities. Another cited the unwholesome effect of "restrictions and espionage" upon young women forced to live in dormitories, where they would be closely supervised and discouraged from developing a sense of responsibility for their own actions. This new rule challenged the integrity of Cornell women, wrote one graduate who stated,

The privileges of Cornell, with the old liberty as to mode of life, have attracted a class of women to whom dictation in matters which beyond question they were best fitted to arrange for themselves, is irksome in the extreme. They are not likely to overlook the fact that a few institutions, notably the University of Michigan, still offer them the higher education with option as to their manner of living. They are not those who do least credit to the University training, but are in many cases those who, having been long dependent upon their own resources, have developed a strength of character and independence of judgment which guarantee the best result of the mental culture they may gain.

In their petition, the alumnae sought to prove the injustice of the regulation by reiterating Ezra Cornell's original intent to found an institution to serve all people without limitation. They pointed out that this law was depriving one group of students, "a class which has not merited the deprivation," of their right to choose their own living arrangements. The trustees were reminded of the commitment, implicit in the original Sage gift, that women would have equal opportunities with men at Cornell University. Under this new rule, they claimed a distinction was being made between men and women which placed unusual restrictions upon women. Attention was called to the many comfortable homes adjacent to the campus in which women students could reside inexpensively and still enjoy a satisfying social life. The graduates reassured the administration that they were in very good health, regardless of their place of residence while in college.

Once delivered to the Board of Trustees, the women's petition vanished, and the compulsory dormitory requirement went into effect. Unfortunately, their impassioned plea for justice was presented to the same trustee meeting which was unexpectedly involved with the resignation of Andrew D. White as university president. Ellen Brown commented later that "they and he had enough to think about without giving ear to our little bleat." [14]

With the establishment of compulsory dormitory residence for women, the university administration did for the first time make a clear distinction in its policy between male and female students. Opportunity would no longer be the same for women and men, but different. President Charles Kendall Adams explained in 1891 that Cornell's policy was based on sex differences and different social roles:

So long as an inflexible public opinion holds young women to more rigid accountability for conduct than it holds young men, it is not wise to disregard the educational power of proper direction and control. . . . It [Cornell University] has never professed, nor does it now profess, that the young women admitted to its classes may indulge with impunity the same freedom that is permitted to young men. . . . It holds that at the age at which at least a very considerable number of young women come to the University, no small part of the education that they need is the elevating influence of a wholesome social atmosphere and the inspiration of a wise and discreet guidance and companionship. It was to secure these ends that a Principal of Sage College was appointed. . . . A vast majority of the young women are not only earnestly devoted to the working out of great and noble purposes, but are also disposed on every occasion to exert their influence in behalf of a cultivated and refined social life. . . . It should be known by all parents that are thinking of sending their daughters to Cornell that Sage College is designed only for those who have sufficient maturity and stability to enable them to understand the spirit of a university and the true nature of university work. [15]

President Adams enunciated the ideology of the era. The late nineteenth century is characterized as a period of affluence and polarization, a time marked by the emergence of an upper class which placed great value on manners and morals, and consequently, as an era when conservative respectability became a primary social goal and repression was common. The differentiation between the sexes which occurred at Cornell merely reflected a predominant social view and adapted university policy to the traditional regulatory attitudes already prevailing at Antioch College and in all the women's colleges. The freedom that Cornell women had previously enjoyed, however, was comparable to the experience of women at the University of Michigan, but women at Michigan were not subjected to social supervision and segregated housing until the turn of the century. Relative to Michigan, the shift of policy at Cornell, from liberal to conservative, particularly when the origins of coeducation are traced back to egalitarian reform movements, was major and paradoxical. Since there is no evidence to suggest that the shift was in any way related to improper behavior among the women, it must be examined to determine the causal factors.

The rule requiring women to live in Sage College was motivated on one hand by economic conditions. Despite the enthusiastic response to its founding, the university experienced increasing financial pressures in the years following the adoption of coeducation. Its original investments failed to produce the anticipated revenue but rather became an added drain on university resources. Some of the men who gave so generously to the university in its early years, such as Ezra Cornell and John McGraw, died. The depression of 1873 and the diminished demand for technical education in a period of limited employment opportunity were important contributors to a sharp decline in enrollment. In 1875, when Sage College opened, the total enrollment of the university was 542. By 1881, it had declined to 384.[16] Added to the economic stringencies of the time, the national de-

bate on the merits of coeducation continued. The enrollment of women students failed to increase and in fact, declined from 67 in 1876 to 59 in 1881.[17] The gift of Sage
College was originally a welcome and needed addition to
the foundering university. As the institution's economic
difficulties mounted, the empty rooms of this elegant edifice became too expensive to maintain in anticipation of a
more favorable social climate for coeducation. Those responsible for university management believed they could
not afford to allow women freedom of choice if Sage College
was to become economically viable.

In addition, there was a decisive shift of power within
the university administration. The influence of Cornell and
White, both staunch advocates of equal opportunity for
women, was declining. After Cornell's death, White became
increasingly restless and distracted from university affairs.
He was often absent from the campus in the late 1870s on
diplomatic missions abroad.

The leadership vacuum was soon filled by Henry Sage,
who had been elected chairman of the Board of Trustees in
1875 and moved permanently to Ithaca in 1877. The ideal-
ism of the founder and the scholarly president was soon
displaced by the authoritarian practicality of the businessman. Eager to achieve status through his association with
distinguished men and an institution of higher education,
Sage had originally echoed and financially supported liberal
views on the place of women in the university. Once committed to the cause of coeducation, his money invested and
his name associated with this controversial experiment,
Sage had a vested interest in making Sage College a success
by any means available. He was not a man who would accept failure.

But Sage's abandonment of liberalism had another more
compelling motivation. His increasing sensitivity to the
need for conservative respectability for himself and Cornell
University can be attributed directly to his close association
with that renowned liberal, Henry Ward Beecher, and indi-

rectly, to the charismatic advocate of free love, Victoria Woodhull. In 1871, Woodhull had publicly charged Beecher, the distinguished religious leader, with adultery with the wife of one of his parishioners, Elizabeth Tilton. The Beecher-Tilton affair became a sensational national scandal, and Sage was directly involved as chairman of the Plymouth Church committee set up to investigate the charges.[18] The committee, composed of men like Sage who had invested heavily in Beecher's various good works and thus were highly dependent upon his reputation, could find no evidence to impair confidence in Beecher or his church. A later court trial in 1875 resulted in a hung jury, but Mrs. Tilton eventually confessed that the charges were true. Woodhull had succeeded in tarnishing Beecher's image as a liberal by revealing his immorality and thus was undoubtedly the prime cause of Sage's withdrawal from liberalism and his need to reaffirm his respectability. Woodhull's shocking revelations caused moral turmoil in Victorian society, divisiveness in the women's rights movement, and in addition, several changes at Cornell University after 1871. Since the university was under continual attack as a godless institution because of its secularism, Sage contributed funds to construct a chapel: he specifically wanted a building which would project an image of "attendance at chapel."[19] Sage's son Dean then endowed the Sage Preacherships, a program to bring outstanding clergy of various denominations but from "strong orthodox faiths" to the campus on a weekly basis, and also provided funds for the Sage Chapel Choir.[20] President White had specifically instructed Professor Burt G. Wilder to provide lectures for students on physiology and hygiene but when Wilder in 1875 composed his text *What Young People Ought to Know,* the Board of Trustees forced him to omit a chapter on birth control.[21] By 1880 it was noted that Sage's sensitivity to respectability had reached a feverish pitch, and Susan Sage doubtless encouraged his return to orthodoxy in regard to women.[22] As a result, Sage's stated belief in liberty for women gave way to an insistence on propriety, supervision, and regulation. With the decline of White's tempering influence, Sage accumulated increasing power and played a crucial role in defining a more limited, differentiated sphere for women at Cornell. Whether Sage intended to protect women benevolently or to confine them maliciously is unclear, but the official title given to the matron of Sage College was for many years "Warden," and in response the Sage residents were often referred to as "inmates."

In contrast to the similarity of opportunity for men and women espoused by White and Cornell, it was the difference between the sexes which determined their experience at Cornell after 1884. Men had few restrictions imposed on their choice of housing, but women were required to live in dormitories or university-approved housing for the next seventy-eight years. While this specialized policy based on the assumed needs of women resulted in superior housing facilities, it had in addition widespread, long-range influence on the experience of women at Cornell.

As a result of the compulsory dormitory requirement, the university assumed two functions in the education of women which it did not perform as extensively for men. The first was to protect women and to supervise their behavior. Carefully selected women, in later years titled "housemothers," were charged with the guidance and supervision of women students. Furthermore, the Women's Self Government Association, an outgrowth of the original women's organization in Sage College, had the legislative power to establish rules and the judicial power to enforce them. Students had extensive responsibility for self-regulation but the ultimate authority rested with the university administration, represented by the Dean of Women. Some rules specified curfews for weeknights and weekends. Others defined proper social behavior, permissible activities, and required chaperonage. Men were allowed to visit women in their dormitories at specified hours—in the parlor or living room only. Restrictions were liberalized

through the years but there were consistently clear cut social limits set for women while few were imposed on men.

The education of women assumed another dimension not
provided for men, which was training in the social graces.
In her report for 1910–1911, Gertrude Shorb Martin, the Adviser of Women, stated that the dormitory, as the college
home of women, should provide the same social training
provided by "the excellent private home." She believed that
the dormitory atmosphere and organized programs should
encourage "a knowledge of the courtesies and social
usages" basic to good manners and also, that "its entertain-
ments should be sufficiently numerous and varied in character to give to all the members of the home a certain indis-
pensable minimum of social experience."[23] For many years,
proper dress and decorum were required for nightly dinners at dormitory tables, with housemothers setting high
standards of dignity and grace. There were teas, receptions,
and dances organized within the various living units. The
Cornell woman was expected to learn to behave like a lady
and often, instructive booklets on campus manners were
distributed to women as they entered the university. Although the university eventually provided dormitories for
men and encouraged the development of fraternities, the
administration rarely intervened to require social experience for men. The regulations imposed on male living
centers were primarily motivated by the desire to maintain
propriety and to protect women, not to encourage male social development.

The policy requiring dormitory residence originated in
the economic need to fill the rooms of Sage College. It remained in effect long after Sage College was filled to capacity and additional dormitories for women had been constructed. Intended as a device to assure parents that Cornell
University was a safe and proper place to send their daughters, with the passage of time this policy maintained its
moral function and in addition, established an absolute
limit on the numbers of women accepted for admission.

Therefore, the admission criteria for women and men were no longer the same.

As the numbers of students competing for admission continually increased, limits on enrollment were necessary and quotas for both sexes were established. Quotas for male applicants were determined by the availability of classroom space. For women, the quotas equaled the number of dormitory spaces available plus the number of approved rooms in Ithaca. The phrase "female beds" was used by both administrators and students to describe the determinant of admission for women.

Cornell's decision to regulate the lives of female students by insisting on university-approved housing for them severely limited the numbers of women admitted and caused the rejection of more women than men, regardless of ability. Urban institutions could utilize alternative facilities near their campuses, but Cornell's location in a small community and its limited capacity to devote funds to dormitory construction restricted the number of female beds. In 1900, women constituted approximately 14 percent of the total student body on the Ithaca campus and did not exceed 25 percent until the 1960s.[24] An unusual combination of privately endowed and publicly supported colleges within a single university makes comparison with other institutions difficult but Cornell compares unfavorably with the most similar institutions, whose student populations include between 27 and 42 percent women.[25]

The low ratio of women to men has influenced other decisions as well. For example, when the Cornell National Scholarship Program was instituted in 1944 to attract promising scholars from a wider geographic area, twenty-five scholarships were awarded annually. Merit, financial need, and capacity for leadership were the influential criteria, with eighteen scholarships earmarked for men, five for women, and two undifferentiated by sex.[26] This determination was based on the proportion of women enrolled in the university at the time and is indicative of the fact that the merit of individual women is consistently superseded by the numerical restrictions imbedded in university policy.

The quota based on the number of female beds available subjected women to more selective admission criteria than were applied for men. Contrary to the original fear that women would lower academic standards, women have consistently excelled because they were more highly selected. One study, initiated at the request of the National Interfraternity Conference, covered the period between 1938 and 1950, with the exception of the war years. According to this study, the averages of undergraduate women consistently exceeded those of undergraduate men.[27] More recently, another study showed that in a College of Arts and Sciences graduating class which was 33 percent female, 40 percent of the honors went to women. In a graduating class of the College of Agriculture which had 15 percent women, 50 percent of the degrees awarded with honors went to women.[28] These studies indicate nothing definitive about the relative intelligence of the sexes, because men and women have not been tested by similar standards or experienced equal opportunity in admission, but reflect instead societal expectations differentiated by sex.

Quotas, based on the number of female beds allotted to each division of the university, became a mechanism for channeling women into fields of study considered appropriate for their sex by a conservative society and university administration. Propriety was the standard of admission, not individual merit or potential. In the early years, the university was a relatively homogenous unit. The nationwide process of specialization and professionalization was evident at Cornell in the late nineteenth century with the formation of special schools and colleges in law, medicine, agriculture, engineering, graduate studies, veterinary medicine, and architecture. Later, schools such as Business and Public Administration, Hotel Administration, and Industrial and Labor Relations were added. Historically, the admission of women to these schools has been severely restricted. As recently as 1966, women constituted less than 1 percent of those admitted to the College of Engineering; to the College of Agriculture, approximately 11 percent; to the Graduate School, 19 percent; to the School of Industrial and Labor Relations, 14 percent; and to the Law School, 2 percent.[29]

As women were largely excluded from the professionally oriented units, their admission to the College of Arts and Sciences was also limited. Since the turn of the century, this unit has grown in numbers of students more than most others in the university while the composition of its student body has remained approximately one-third female.[30] Despite the proven academic excellence of women students, their opportunity for admission to this college has been less than equal. Of particular relevance is the fact that access to an area of intellectual development generally regarded as not sex related was determined on the basis of sex. The restrictive policies toward female admissions, expressed through the female bed quotas for the College of Arts and Sciences, reflected a limited view of women's potential in the face of increasing emphasis on science, research, and professionalism.

The pursuit of a Cornell education was reserved primarily for men and then an alternative evolved for women. Home economics began its rise at Cornell University in 1900 as part of the wider movement to improve domestic life through education and the application of science, and was closely related to the growth of agricultural education. If the work of the man on the farm could be made more effective through education, then some like Professor Liberty Hyde Bailey of Cornell's College of Agriculture believed it was equally important to extend educational programs to rural women. The reading courses for farmer's wives, conceptualized by Bailey and inaugurated by Martha Van Rensselaer, had expanded by 1925 into a comprehensive program in the College of Home Economics that aimed to uplift the quality of food, clothing, shelter, and family life. The College of Home Economics, the first nationally to be subsidized by a state, did provide opportunities for women. Here highly selected, able women from diverse backgrounds were able to obtain a state-subsidized education which had both a domestic and a professional orientation. In fact, this college emphasized vocational preparation and provided career guidance for its students at a time when the assumption was made in most other academic units that undergraduate women were destined only for marriage. For countless numbers of women, home economics afforded excellent preparation for their lives in the home and in the labor force.

The fact must be recognized, however, that home economics also served other purposes. Derived from the as-

Early students in the College of Home Economics learn techniques of food preparation. The elementary nature of their task belies the strong scientific foundation of the curriculum and its vocational orientation. Courses in home economics evolved into a multifaceted program of teaching, research, and extension activities, which in recent years has been renamed the College of Human Ecology. (Cornell University, DMUA.)

sumed needs and interests of women, it was a means of removing women from the academic and professional mainstream. Many talented women, who might have become scientists and mathematicians, were counseled to study home economics—the appropriate place for women. Home economics training offered the potential for improving American home and family life, which is always of vital importance, but it also reaffirmed woman's traditional place in the domestic sphere. Cornell's admissions policies reflected this conservative view so that sex, rather than ability, did determine educational opportunities. Strict segregation of the sexes was maintained; only women were admitted to home economics and only men were permitted to prepare themselves in such fields as engineering and law.

The disparity between the numbers of females and males, perpetuated through admissions quotas, has created a skewed social environment on the campus, has kept women in the position of a minority group, and has exaggerated the differences between the sexes. The first women students, although strong-minded, were invaders in traditionally male territory. It was not only their numerical inferiority but doubtless their single-minded determination to prove themselves and their success in doing so which contributed to the development of a strong tradition of anticoedism at Cornell. The initial antagonism to women students was intensified by later developments.

In the late 1880s, the university's character was moderated, changing from a free-spirited experiment into a mirror of conservative Victorian society. As the professionally oriented units of the university expanded, the men who came as students were no longer the poor sons of upstate farmers but were increasingly the sons of wealthy men who came from urban centers to study engineering, law, and architecture. At the same time, the women who had the temerity to attend Cornell were often those of limited means, determined to secure professional training as teachers. The men were not only numerically superior but they banded

Coeds of the 1890s and later, who looked much like other women, were the subject of derogatory songs, popular on campus for many years. Male students sang, "I'm glad all the girls are not like Cornell women, They're ugly as sin and there's no good within 'em" or "The coed leads a wretched life, She eats potatoes with a knife." As skirts grew shorter, the women of Cornell reputedly had the ugliest legs in the East. (Cornell University, DMUA.)

together to form one of the most extensively developed fraternity systems in the country. These fraternities became a dominant influence in campus life; they set the tone of the community, and their palatial residences served as major centers of social activity. Furthermore, as the men of Cornell sought to equal Harvard and Yale in academic, social, and professional prestige, the presence of women, they thought, severely diminished this possibility. As Victorian society became polarized, so did the college campus, where the social chasm between men and women became wider and more rigidly structured.

In 1894, the *New York Herald* published a widely read account of social life at Cornell and reported the opinion of one faculty member who said, "There can be no doubt that the large proportion of them (the coeds) are entitled to no social recognition whatever. Most of them are hard students, and some are really brilliant intellectually, but their personal appearance and conduct in general show unmistakably that they would be out of place in fashionable college society."[31] By unwritten law, the women of Cornell were definitely out of plące. While campus organizations discouraged the participation of women, the fraternities categorically excluded Cornell women from social events. Fraternities would not allow their members to speak to women students on the campus, to invite them to parties, or to consider giving a Cornell woman a fraternity pin. The punishment for such transgressions ranged from being forced into the shower, to fines and the removal of fraternity pins from the men. Some fraternities persisted in this anticoed pose until the mid-1920s when the first coeds were permitted to attend parties. The tradition of charging a man an extra fee to bring a Cornell woman to a party and of symbolic voting on whether a particular Cornell woman could be included in a houseparty continued in some groups until the 1950s.[32]

Ellen Coit Brown '82 reported that "we never talked to the men in the halls or the classrooms when coming and going, nor walked anywhere with them—on the campus. In the large lecture halls and the small classrooms, filled mostly with our brothers and cousins and future husbands, we walked demurely, as inconspicuously as we could manage, and took seats, always at the front. . . . We were not insulted—only tolerated and ignored." The class pictured here met in 1910, but the seating patterns had not changed in thirty years. (Cornell University, DMUA.)

Cloistered in Sage College and excluded from most campus activities, women formed their own organizations and social activities within the dormitory. Student government, a drama club, an orchestra, sororities, and honor societies exclusively for women flourished for years, and women were sensitive to the fact that their place at Cornell was an inferior one. One woman observed in 1892: "President Schurman gave an opening address yesterday noon to all the students and his talk was very fine, although he said rather more to the men students than to the women students."[33]

In his *History of Cornell,* Morris Bishop stated that after the 1920s, the old tradition of anticoedism faded away and the women students were eventually fully integrated into Cornell life.[34] On the contrary, I would suggest that many of the patterns of segregation, established in the early years, have been maintained through time. Based strictly on the numerical disparity between men and women, Cornell University has remained a male-oriented institution, and the male ethos has prevailed. Women have been kept in their place.

As an example of the separate and unequal experience of women, the class organizations demonstrate the consistency of this pattern because they have been important vehicles for student and alumni activity throughout the university's history. In the early years, a few singularly intrepid women of Sage College persisted in exercising their rights as class members by attending the annual class supper. Their efforts provoked heated debate. Since women had already gained access to some minor campus clubs, the men were incensed when women attempted to attend the major social event of the year. In 1879, a male student asked, "Are not the peculiar advantages of association of men with men weighty enough to cause a need here of some organizations not wholly coeducational in character?"[35] If the women continued to attend, the men feared that the entire nature of the class supper might have to be changed. A woman student replied to these arguments:

This is dreadfully revolutionary and exciting; class suppers should go on in the old way by all means; while there is constant improvement in such minor things as science, art and letters, a matter of such mighty import as the class supper should be permitted to retain its "long-established character". . . . What a blood-curdling state of affairs! How much more meet and becoming it would be for these ambitious dames to eschew Christian associations and literary societies, and content themselves with the Navy balls, where there is not the slightest impropriety in the close embraces of a waltz and polka.[36]

Another male student joined in the debate by stating that, although he admired those who braved public opinion to stand up for a principle, he wondered whether the principle involved in attending class suppers was sufficient "to justify that strain upon a young girl's peculiar beauty—her maidenly modesty and reserve—which attendance upon class suppers must necessitate."[37] The classes remained separate organizations for men and women.

In 1900, Mollie Crawford, a sixteen-year-old freshmen who later became a physician and university trustee, learned of the organizing meeting of the Class of 1904, but when she and a group of Sage women attended, they found their presence was not considered appropriate. Once again the merits of segregation of the sexes in class organizations and indeed the whole issue of coeducation was called into question. A university trustee proclaimed the proposed change too radical a reformation of established tradition. While he regarded Cornell's women with great pride, particularly since experience had proven that coeducation had not caused them to become "non-womanly," he did believe that the women of Cornell should be protected from any possibility of discourtesy. President Jacob Gould Schurman reminded the students that coeducation was the settled policy of the university and that the spirit of equality must be considered in all matters falling outside the jurisdiction of the administration, but that this was a matter to be decided by the students.[38]

For the next sixty years, each entering class continued to be organized on the basis of sex, with separate officers and activities. After graduation, men and women maintained separate alumni class organizations, separate reunion programs, and separate columns of class news in the *Cornell Alumni News*. In 1951, when the suggestion was made by the senior class that the alumni classes might be combined in the interest of economy, this idea was vetoed by officials as too severe a departure from established tradition, which was based, they said, on the different interests of men and women.[39] For many years, when the alumni organized programs to interest high school students in attending Cornell, only males were invited. At graduation, the alumni usually presented an award to the outstanding senior—a man.

Cornell clubs, organized across the country to maintain alumni interest, were also strictly segregated by sex. Efforts to hold joint programs were not without friction, as one woman reported: "I am used to the bad taste of the stag dinners here and it was tried in the First Alumni Convocation here, but we really foiled that. We were offered seats in the balcony which we refused on the ground that we were alumni also. The committee capitulated and the matter was settled here and in the future."[40] The Cornell Women's Clubs are well organized, active in student recruitment, and maintain an impressive scholarship fund for women, but the disparity in numbers between men and women has limited their effectiveness as a force for change in the status of women at the university.

Shaped by the social climate and the unequal sex ratio of Cornell, women learned that it was more important to be charming, feminine, and passive, than to be intelligent and aggressive. When fraternities finally abandoned social ostracism of Cornell women, which some did not give up until after World War II, the social climate was equally negative in many respects. Social activity was extensive and highly organized, based largely on planned events of a formal nature. Weekend dates were very important and attendance at special occasions, such as university dances and fraternity houseparties was a crucial measure of social success. The Cornell woman found a premium placed upon her social desirability, not her intelligence. The situation was frustrating for both sexes. Extreme pressure was exerted on the most attractive women as prospective dates and those who were not able to compete socially or did not choose to were regarded as feminine failures. Men too were placed in a very competitive situation as they sought to win the favor of the scarce, highly coveted women. Some alumnae recalled, in 1972, their reaction to campus sociality: [41]

Because there were so few women in my school, I necessarily became a little brash in my association with men students.

Coeducation probably resulted in less attention to academics than if I had been in a women's college. . . . I can think of how it reinforced my socialization regarding women's roles.

As a young woman of slender means who had attended a a girls' high school where academic accomplishment was stressed, I was rather unattractive, I should say. I had a few dates. I met men with the assurance that I was meeting them on equal ground and not originally with the idea of attracting them sexually. Of course, that aspect was important. I like men and I like physically attractive men, but the Cornell of the thirties was too unbalanced in male-female proportions with the result that the importance of dating was exaggerated.

The usual 1950s profound sense of being an inferior misfit. So few dates! No social life! I think I shocked everybody by going out alone on Saturday night—good girls stayed in the dorm so nobody would know they didn't have dates. I would perhaps have been happier at a girl's school. At any rate, conformity, particularly to social roles, was a constant problem. . . . We all disliked it. My friends and I wanted badly to be "masculine" in mind while immensely socially popular. And, of course, our sexual misinformation was massive and the horror of pregnancy endemic. It's surprising what adolescents can live through. It was dreadful, actually.

These comments represent more than a few isolated, dissatisfied women—they illustrate an uneasiness with the artificiality and rigidity of the social experience reflected in other studies.[42] The social contest was unequal, artificially out of balance, and an extremely powerful force in maintaining women in their traditional social role. Certainly, the emphasis on social life and the pressure it exerted on women is similar to that described in the studies of Matina Horner as depressive of the motive to achieve.[43] Cornell women learned to be quietly pleased by election to Phi Beta Kappa but noisily elated over pinning to a fraternity man or an engagement. The cultural message which the Cornell experience reinforced for both men and women, was that woman's proper role is as a social appendage to a man.

At the same time, there has been little specific research related to the effects of this social imbalance on men but there must have been male students who, aspiring to social as well as academic success, were placed at a severe disadvantage by the shortage of women. Many, particularly those who were personally insecure or who lacked the social advantages of fraternity life, were almost doomed to continual rebuffs from women and, one must assume, subsequent deflation of their sense of self-esteem. Men could complete their Cornell years having had only limited contacts with women and little social experience, either through lack of interest or, more likely, through the inability to meet successfully the rigorous tests of social competition.

The Cornell environment encouraged women to compete socially but it discouraged them from competing physically. In athletic activities, the women of Cornell did not compete seriously—they played. The health and physical development of women were major concerns at the time of their admission to Cornell. This concern however has not been expressed in reality. Despite the vigor with which Cornell women played basketball and rowed on a crew in the 1890s, the twentieth century brought two changes on the national athletic scene and at Cornell which superseded the original focus on health. As large scale intercollegiate athletic competition developed rapidly for men, the idea that athletic competition was unwise and even unfeminine for women gained acceptance. Men's sports became more competitive, as women's sports were taken less seriously and focused primarily on intramural activities and annual "playdays." The dominance of male athletics and male athletes in the Cornell experience is reflected in the pages of the yearbook, *The Cornellian*. In 1935, seventy-two pages were devoted to male athletes, competitions, and athletic organizations whereas one page was devoted to similar activities for women. Likewise, in 1951, stories about male athletics consumed sixty pages whereas women's required only one.

Proud, determined oarswomen organized the Women's Boating Club in 1897. Emily Dunning Barringer '97 (*seated, middle of second row*) and Nan Gilbert Seymour '97 (*top row, second from left in male attire*) later became physicians. Varsity coach Charles E. Courtney (*seated*) and varsity coxswain Frederick Colson (*standing, left*) encouraged their spirited efforts. (Cornell University, DMUA.)

Few people believed in 1950 that women could or should row. The idea of women rowing in competition was so preposterous that, as a joke, the author and friends borrowed a shell and entered the Interfraternity Boat Race on Beebe Lake. (Author's photograph.)

Such a measure is only superficially indicative of the difference in staff, buildings, equipment, and funding provided to foster the physical development of men and women. Women were not only discouraged from competition with other women, but were categorically excluded from even marginal participation at male athletic events as cheerleaders or members of the Big Red Band, both important components of the athletic program. Woman's place in Cornell sports was in the bleachers as admiring spectators of male athletic prowess.

The Cornell experience also reinforced the traditional concept that women should be followers, not leaders, of men. Within the segregated organizations, such as the women's government association, sororities, and clubs, the female student did have ample incentive and opportunity to develop leadership skills. Outside of these groups, however, women were excluded from attaining one of the major goals of a university education: the training to be future leaders. Most major campus organizations—the newspaper, the

After many years of low expectations and limited funding, women's athletic activities began to be taken seriously in the 1970s. Ellis H. Robinson
'18 and C. Edward Murray '14 presented the first shell given specifically to
the women's crew for intercollegiate competition. (Cornell University, Office of Public Information.)

yearbook, the student union, and the united religious organization—were dominated by men until World War II and maintained separate auxiliaries for women. Some organizational structures were less rigid than others, but generally women were confined in marginal positions. The predominance of men and the strength of the fraternity system in developing campus leaders precluded opportunity for women. Not until the early 1940s, when the campus had few civilian men and was devoted to the training of military units, were women were able to attain power in the direction of campus affairs. During the war years, women assumed direction of almost all major campus organizations and publications, and as late as 1949 held important leadership positions. There was support at the time for this unusual situation because women, unaffected by the demand for military service, were the most stable members of the campus community to give continuity to student organizations. As the campus returned to normalcy after the war, male students approached the Dean of Men for advice on the proper strategy to remove women from these positions of power. New patterns of leadership then developed; some women were able to rise above the office of secretary to become vice president or cochairmen, but rarely president.[44]

The model of leadership set by the faculty, the administration, and the Board of Trustees was almost exclusively male. M. Elizabeth Tidball has documented the importance of female role models in institutional leadership as a crucial factor encouraging feminine achievement.[45] Throughout Cornell history, there have been few role models for women.

In 1874, Ezra Cornell assured a woman who inquired about a position as Cornell professor, "There is no law or usage that will prevent the appointment of a woman to a professorship—Merit [sic] as a teacher will be the test." He asserted that the university needed and wanted the best professors available, regardless of sex, religion, politics, nationality, or color.[46] Many years passed before the trustees and faculty were able to identify "the best" women to become Cornell professors. A few women worked in the scientific laboratories and in the 1890s, a woman was appointed to supervise physical education for female students. The first to teach in a Cornell classroom was Louise S. Brownell who, in 1897, was the Warden of Sage College and also a lecturer on English literature. Her proposed appointment to the rank of assistant professor provoked so much resistance among the trustees that action was deferred, Brownell eventually withdrew her name, and in 1900, resigned from the university. In 1898, Anna Comstock's name was proposed as assistant professor of nature study and she did become the first woman to achieve faculty rank. Her appointment was awarded for the summer session, however, and in the fall of 1899 was rescinded because of trustee opposition. A nationally recognized authority in her field, Comstock was not accorded even the lowest faculty rank for thirteen years and did not become a full professor until 1920.

It was through the growth of home economics that women were eventually accorded faculty status. At the turn of the century, Martha Van Rensselaer came to Cornell to work on an educational program for rural women and in 1907, was joined by Flora Rose, who was to become her coworker in developing the Department of Home Economics. Even though the Board of Trustees supported this project, they resisted granting faculty rank to the two women, who were designated only as lecturers. Debate continued within the Board and the faculty until 1911 when the title of professor was conferred on Van Rensselaer and Rose, making them Cornell's first women professors. It was suggested by the director of the College of Agriculture, however, that they refrain from attending faculty meetings until the opposition to their appointments had subsided.[47]

In the years that followed, women were reluctantly welcomed as Cornell faculty members, with few exceptions, only in the College of Home Economics. In other units of the university, most women remained confined in the lowest levels of academic employment as lecturers and assistants. In the College of Arts and Sciences, the unit which has historically educated the most women, no woman achieved the position of assistant professor before 1947 and none gained the rank of full professor until after 1960.[48] At least eighty-six years passed after Ezra Cornell wrote the letter that proclaimed merit as the most important criterion for selection as a Cornell professor before a woman was deemed worthy of a professorship in this college.

Discrimination against women faculty has been clearly documented in major colleges and universities. In regard to this common employment practice, the behavior of those at Cornell has been particularly interesting. There are few institutions which have been willing to train women for high level research and teaching, and the numbers of women with doctoral degrees are relatively small when compared with men. Despite the slight representation of women at the graduate level, Cornell is placed among the leading institutions which have facilitated such training for women. This university ranked among the leading institutions which awarded doctorates to outstanding women in science before 1920.[49] It stands in the forefront of institutions which for years have been most productive of women scholars, those undergraduate women who later earned doctorates.[50] The inclusion of home economics graduates in such calculations and the role of this college as a national center for graduate study in home economics doubtless inflates Cornell's standing relative to other institutions but it does maintain a dominant position. The university has historically fulfilled a paradoxical mission—to permit women to learn but not to teach.

The general reluctance to employ women on the faculty became solidified in policies which prohibited the immediate hiring of Cornell graduates without intervening experience elsewhere. An effort to prevent intellectual inbreeding, this policy worked a particular hardship on women who had earned Cornell degrees, were married, and whose homes and families were in Ithaca. The antinepotism policy, in effect for many years, deprived the university of highly competent women with doctorates, if their husbands were already members of the faculty. Many of these women, limited in the opportunity for alternative employment in Ithaca, labored for years in low-level positions, as research associates or as secretaries, for which they were definitely overqualified. For example, Eleanor J. Gibson, who earned the M.S. at Smith College in 1933 and a Ph.D. at Yale University in 1938, was an assistant professor of psychology on the Smith College faculty when it became important in 1949 to move to the Cornell campus in the interest of her husband's academic career. Because of the antinepotism rule, she was able to pursue her own scholarly interests at Cornell only in the capacity of a research associate. Over the years, as she achieved reknown through her work and her leadership in professional organizations, Eleanor Gibson conducted her own research and supervised the work of graduate students; but, without faculty rank, she was not technically qualified to sign her own name as the person who had supervised doctoral research.[51] The many talents of this woman were not wasted at Cornell, but they were not fully utilized or given proper recognition.

In the early days, Andrew D. White as president directed the faculty and staff single-handed. With expansion in the student body and the curriculum, and the establishment of separate schools and colleges, a complex administrative hierarchy of deans, vice presidents, and other officials has continually been extended to support the president. Historically, the only administrative positions held by women were the deanship of the College of Human Ecology and that of Warden of Sage College, a post later titled Adviser or Dean of women. At the administrative level of the university, men made decisions—women served as secretaries.

Likewise, few women have been able to influence university policy through membership on the Board of Trustees. One of the innovations espoused by Cornell and White was a board representing a diversity of interests, free from domination by any religious group or other faction. As the number of trustees increased from the first seventeen to more than forty-five on the board by 1960, members were elected by the board, the alumni, the faculty, and from agricultural and labor groups in the state, with officials of the state government serving ex officio. The eldest male lineal descendant of Ezra Cornell is automatically a member. The first woman to serve on the Board, M. Carey Thomas, was elected in 1895.[52] Succeeding her in later years were others who were consistently the "token" women on the board. The Cornell alumnae made repeated efforts to elect others, but the overwhelming ratio of men to women made the election of women impossible. Both Anna Comstock and Kate Gleason were defeated. Mollie Crawford was twice defeated before she won election in 1927. She was again defeated for later reappointment, a defeat she attributed to the feeling of certain members that having two women on the board was "a dangerous thing."[53] Judge Mary Donlon served on the board for twenty-nine years and was the first woman chosen to serve on its Executive Committee. There was never more than one woman at a time until 1944. Two women served consecutively until 1947 when a third joined them. From 1895 to 1960, ten women in all served as trustees elected by the alumni, one was elected by the faculty, and only one of these women, Mary Donlon, was later reelected by the board itself. Because of the close ties between the university and the state government, the Governor has the power to appoint members to the board, but no woman has ever been appointed.[54]

In 1912, Gertrude Martin, the Adviser of Women, challenged the university's attitude toward its women students. She noted in her annual report "an unwillingness to admit that the institution is really and permanently committed to the policy of coeducation; the feeling that the presence of

Mary Donlon LL.B. '20, lawyer and federal judge, is shown in her official role as university trustee at commencement with Trustee Jansen Noyes Jr. '39 (*left*) and President Dale Corson. Her credo that every successful woman should provide "a strong pair of shoulders" on which other women could climb was expressed through her personal example, her active encouragement of other women, and her constant campaigns on behalf of the women of Cornell. (Cornell University, Office of Public Information.)

women somehow renders it inferior to the other great eastern universities . . . a determination to keep it in curriculum and atmosphere as distinctly a man's institution as possible."[55] Mrs. Martin's critical comments remained valid for the next half century.

The original decision to compel women students to reside in Sage College had economic origins and was determined by the dominant, paternalistic views of Henry Sage. That this ruling remained in effect for so many years and was such a significant influence in determining woman's place at Cornell, and her educational and social experience as well, reflected the increasing ideological commitment of society to the sex-differentiated needs, interests, and abilities of individuals. As the years passed, the Cornell community acceded to these social pressures rather than attempting to implement the original egalitarian ideals of the founders. When compared with other institutions in terms of the options provided for individual development unrelated to gender, Cornell University had become by 1960 a place where women had the least possibility for equal opportunity. This condition contrasts sharply with the era of its founding when it surpassed most other colleges and universities in providing similar opportunity for both sexes.[56] Although the Cornell academic world purported to be the bastion of liberalism, it reinforced the most conservative social and occupational roles for women.

To prove that the tradition of anticoedism had passed away and the lives of Cornell men and women had become more congruent, Morris Bishop in his *History of Cornell* quoted a study showing that 38 percent of the married women graduates of the Classes of 1919, 1920, and 1921 had married Cornell men.[57] This supposedly happy ending to the Cornell educational experience was, I suggest, the inevitable result of university policy. Once the university made the decision requiring women to live in dormitories while men did not, the opportunity offered to women was no longer the same but different, not equal but unequal. As

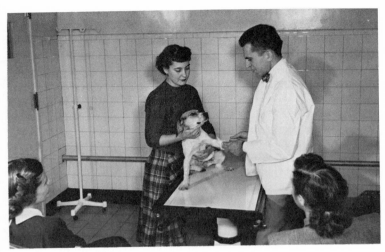

For many years the female bed quota system restricted the number of women admitted to the College of Veterinary Medicine. In 1954 evening classes were held to prepare wives of students to help in their husbands' practices. After four years of instruction, a wife could assist as anesthetist, accountant, animal feeder, and laboratory technician. (Cornell University, DMUA; C. Hadley Smith.)

men were encouraged to become intelligent, competent workers and leaders, most women were prepared for more limited roles as educated wives and mothers. After decades of coeducation, in which women had proven their physical and intellectual ability to achieve an education in a university with men and dominated by men, the end result adhered more closely to Rousseau's goal of educating women for men, rather than Harriet Mill's ideal of educating women for themselves and for society.

Epilogue

We deny the right of any portion of the species to decide for another portion, or any individual for another individual, what is or is not their proper sphere. The proper sphere for all human beings is the largest and highest which they are able to attain to. What this is cannot be ascertained without complete liberty of choice.

Harriet Taylor Mill
Enfranchisement of Women

The great and leading principle is the absolute and essential importance of human development in its richest diversity.

John Stuart Mill, quoted
in Cornell University's
Plan of Organization, 1866

Before women were admitted to Cornell University, the students had worried and asked, "When all the women get to be students in Cornell University and doctors and lawyers and ministers and brokers, who is to do the childbearing?"[1] Certainly there is little evidence to suggest that the founders of the university intended to initiate revolutionary changes in the relationship between the sexes. Ezra Cornell and Andrew D. White did not envision that the opportunity for higher education would induce all women to forego marriage and motherhood in order to pursue careers. Shaped by an era of egalitarian thought and by a region particularly sensitive to human rights, their objective was to provide a new mode of education as a source of individual perfection, increased options for economic independence, and of societal improvement. With great faith in the ability of individuals to integrate educational opportunity and to regulate their own lives, Cornell and White believed there should be no restriction in higher education based on sex.

The revolution in sex roles, feared by male students, has not occurred. Coeducation, as it evolved for women at Cornell, has not provided them similar experience with men but rather has functioned to construct another set of social barriers confining most of them in woman's traditionally limited sphere. To assume that these barriers were stable and absolute for a period of over seventy-five years, from 1884 until the 1960s, appears simplistic. There was however little change in the broad outlines of the restrictive pattern affecting the campus life of Cornell women throughout this lengthy period. The fact that women were regarded differently from men was implicit in the decision that female students must be protected and supervised in university-approved housing, a ruling which confined them as a numerical minority. From this restriction flowed other discrepancies in curriculum, career orientation, leadership training, and athletic experience. Cornell's women remained a privileged, protected group whose special interests were reputedly far different from those of men.

The abandonment by Henry Sage of liberal egalitarian goals in favor of conservative tradition and sexual differentiation was indicative of social trends which shaped the future of women at Cornell University. The university had its origins in the wide ranging critique by Elizabeth Cady Stanton and Susan B. Anthony of all social constraints which confined women in a separate limited sphere. These two women aimed for reform of all legal, economic, political, and social institutions which maintained women under a defect of sex. To Carey Thomas, this was the Egyptian darkness which she believed in 1924 had been dispelled by the admission of women to colleges and universities and to the electorate.

It became evident that such was not the case. The evolution of science, particularly the social sciences, and the dissemination of scientific information did not diminish the effect of former constraints but rather served to support and strengthen them in the twentieth century. Investigations in psychology, sociology, physiology, and biology provided proof which validated traditional concepts. The data mounted from analyses of the human body, from studies of primitive tribes and primate behavior, and from tests of intelligence and aptitudes to prove that sex was a universal differential. From the studies of Cornell's Professor Burt G. Wilder, in which he attempted to relate brain size to in-

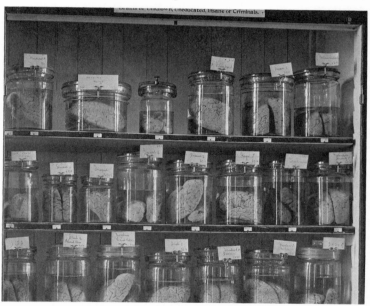

Professor Burt G. Wilder was one of several scientists in the late nineteenth century who attempted to correlate brain size with intelligence. Helen H. Gardener, an author and feminist, objected to some studies which utilized measurable size differentials as proof that women were intellectually inferior to men. Claiming that only the brains of women criminals and paupers had been analyzed, she willed her own brain to the Wilder collection to provide a superior female specimen for research, but her efforts to secure the brain of Elizabeth Cady Stanton for Cornell were unsuccessful. (Cornell University, DMUA.)

telligence and found that the female brain was usually smaller and presumably less functional, to the monumental influence of Sigmund Freud, evidence appeared to establish sex differences. That such research was done primarily by men was little noted.[2]

Scientific data that emphasized sex differences, rather than similarities, served to reinforce separate spheres of activity for men and women. Industrialization and urbanization had already widened the gap by removing gainful employment from the home and increasing the distance between the different worlds of males and females. The sexual dualism of society did have economic origins, as Thorstein B. Veblen, a graduate student in economics at Cornell in 1891, later wrote in his provocative analysis, *The Theory of the Leisure Class*.[3] Veblen delineated the separate economic functions for each sex. The male labored outside the home: the female remained at home to live in leisure. As he produced, she was the consumer of goods. The man aimed for achievement and power while the woman lived vicariously and through her clothing, her home, and her activities, served as a critical measure of her husband's success. In this theoretical framework, woman remained outside the sphere of economic productivity and was most honored for her lack of effort. Coupled with economic theory, the scientific evidence of sex differentials in intelligence, personality traits, and aptitudes refuted the arguments of reformers for equal educational and professional opportunity for women.

Instead, the twentieth-century woman was identified as the possessor of special female attributes and a particular feminine mission. Suffragists and social reformers, who earlier had based their campaigns on the need for equal justice for women, now claimed that women could save not only the home and family but the total society. The purifying force of the moral superiority of women, they asserted, would cleanse society of political corruption and economic exploitation. Those who, like Florence Kelley, sought to improve the lot of working women campaigned not for equality but for protective labor legislation based on the special needs of women.

That conservative views on the abilities and social function of women remained powerful for so many years on the Cornell campus is attributable to the deceptive nature of the new theories that were propounded. Ideas that appeared to offer modern wisdom and a fresh perspective actually perpetuated ancient constraints. New scientific and economic information which emanated from learned experts was taught in the classrooms and discussed in the dormitories. Women and men incorporated these ideas into their social expectations, their campus behavior, and their life plans.

The effect of the new knowledge was to reaffirm woman in her separate domestic world. For most women, it was assumed that the purpose of acquiring a college education was not to prepare for a lengthy career but to become an educated wife and mother. Catharine Beecher's glorification of domesticity came to fruition in the home economics movement, in which Cornell University was a dominant force after 1900. Through this course of study, women could apply science and technology to domestic problems; they could become efficient home managers and intelligent consumers; and their educational achievements would in no way threaten the sexual division of labor or of power.

The dichotomy between female and male was further emphasized by changing manners and morals. The barriers to social and sexual pleasure fell: those excluding women from economic and professional endeavors remained strong. Presumptions of progress were misplaced for the new emphasis on sexual freedom served only to entice women ultimately into traditional roles as wives and mothers. They gained the right to be social appendages and sexual partners but not to be equal participants in society.

Added to the social pressures of the first two decades, there was in the 1930s economic impetus for the return to domesticity. The Depression accelerated public disapproval of working women, caused a decline in opportunities for women to obtain college training and employment, and reinforced the belief that woman's most important function was to serve husband and family within the home.[4]

Conservatism toward women received additional support from the men who dominated university governance and from the growing numbers of male graduates. These alumni, many bound together by common experience on the athletic field and in the fraternity house, contributed their time and money generously to preserve the institution as they knew and loved it. The university was also dependent upon public support for financial contributions and to attract promising students. As the statutory colleges became increasingly vital parts of the university, it was ever more dependent upon the state government. The strong ties which developed to a conservative constituency caused sexist traditionalism to flourish in rural isolation.

During the second half century of its history, the university acted to meet the needs of womanly women, not those who might become strong-minded. New programs perpetuated traditional concepts instead of providing unconventional options for women. The university's home economics program was so well regarded and so popular that by 1925, it became a separate college and soon had its own specially designed building to facilitate the expansion of the curriculum. When a new women's dormitory, Balch Hall, was constructed in the 1920s to provide additional housing facilities, it was generously endowed for the benefit of women students and provided more amenities for gracious living and social experience. In Balch, women lived enshrined in ladylike splendor.

The construction of Willard Straight Hall, the student union, is illustrative of the conflict of liberal and conservative views on the place of women at Cornell. Dorothy Whitney Straight carried out the wishes of her husband, Willard D. '01, specified in his will, to use part of his wealth to make Cornell University "a more human place." She determined that construction of a student union would be the most appropriate memorial and that provision of a central social center for all students was most needed. Campus interest in this exciting proposal was intense and many suggestions were offered as to the manner of its execution. But Dorothy Straight, an activist in the suffrage movement, the Women's Trade Union League, the Junior League, and the League of Women Voters, was disconcerted to encounter strong faculty opposition to the inclusion of women. Said one important professor, "Our whole country is today in danger of being run by women. On no account should the coeds be allowed anywhere near such a building."[5] Determined that women students should be able to enjoy the new facility, Straight visited the few existing student unions on other campuses and found that while some did exclude women, others permitted them access through a special entrance. Finally, appearing to offer a compromise, the plans for the construction of Willard Straight Hall provided two entrances, the larger central one for men and a smaller side entrance for women, but Dorothy Straight and the architect had a more far-reaching plan in mind. Once inside the building, they expected that the passage of women to the central area where newspapers, magazines, and tickets to campus events would be sold would soon effect integration of the structure. This objective took longer to accomplish at Cornell than they anticipated. When the building opened in 1925, women were restricted to the use of two lounges and a restroom near the women's entrance. Ten years later, they gained access to the food service areas. During World War II, women finally achieved full use of Willard Straight Hall with one exception, the barber shop.[6] In 1977, over a half century after it opened, the Straight provided hair care for both sexes and thus was fully integrated.

The Cornell experience conveyed through its curriculum, through its admissions, housing, and social policies, and through employment practices, the wisdom of the ages as devised by men. The tenets that there were extreme differences between the sexes and that men and women had clearly defined and different purposes in life for which they must be educated remained strong. The university's concentration on the educational, professional, and athletic needs of white males prevailed. The crusading spirit which had motivated earlier women faded and most accepted their college experience, limited though it was relative to that of men, with equanimity and gratitude. There were few public objections. Students, repeatedly assured that they were privileged to be part of one of the social institutions exemplifying democratic ideals, hesitated to raise objections to a system which was widely approved and which many found socially pleasurable. One woman remembered her days as a coed in the 1940s and said, "I enjoyed coeducation enormously. I took the anti-coed attitude which prevailed in some places for granted. I knew they were wrong but it didn't stir me to action as it might have if I were in school during these feminist days."[7] A former fraternity man, when questioned about his fraternity's practice of charging members an extra fee to bring a Cornell woman to a houseparty in the 1950s, recalled "being troubled by the practice, considering it an anachronism and unbelievably insulting." Few voices were raised to protest the practice at the time.[8]

On the occasions when women did urge change and liberalized opportunities for their sex, the reply from the university administration was not surprising. Increased opportunity for women was impossible and unwarranted from the university's point of view for three reasons. First, the numbers of women admitted could not be increased because there were insufficient female beds available and women were not permitted to live outside the dormitories. Second, women did not use their education as fully as men did but seemed to prefer marriage and motherhood. Third, women did not contribute as generously to the university as men did.[9] The circularity of this argument is clear when the history of women at Cornell and the role of the university in determining the scope and the direction of the female experience is known. As an important contributor to the social process of shaping women for roles as economically dependent wives, the university did indeed share responsibility for the low status of women.

The fallacy of these arguments is seen even more clearly in an earlier period of university history. During its first half century of existence, Cornell University produced an unusual group of women graduates who were distinguished by their varied achievements in the fields of education, scientific research, social reform, medicine, and business. It was also one of the few institutions training women to a high level of proficiency in the sciences. Despite the proven record of serious purpose and the recognized accomplishments of these women, the university did not reduce its resistance to women nor lower the barriers constructed against them. The ratio of women did not increase appreciably, women did not gain entry to the traditionally male fields of study nor did they gain access to faculty rank or positions in the administration.

Between 1950 and 1970, there were social forces building up in America and on the campus which produced a climate conducive to change. The postwar students, sensitive to the issues of individual freedom and social justice, once again began to debate the meaning of the word "persons" and determined to eliminate bias from the campus community. Beginning in the 1950s, fraternities and sororities abolished restrictive policies against Jews and blacks. By 1965, the university responded to civil rights pressures with a commitment to include more black and disadvantaged students.

In the quest for social justice, individual women questioned the restrictive policies affecting their freedom. Curfews for women students gradually disappeared between 1962 and 1969. The residence requirement for women, uniformly imposed in 1884, was gradually liberalized through the 1960s so that, by 1969, the dormitory policies were the same for men and women. The final removal of the residen-

tial requirement resulted not entirely from changing morality but from the same economic pressures which had caused
its imposition. Given increasing freedom to determine their
own residence, students were reluctant to live in dormitories and preferred the independence of apartments off campus. Dormitories were once again standing empty and
maintaining them was economically untenable. A ban on
campus parking hastened the return of a student genera-

In the 1970s women and men enjoy similar housing facilities, similar din-
ing arrangements, and have similar responsibility for their own actions.
Informality and openness now characterize their friendships and social
relationships. (Cornell University, Office of Public Information.)

tion, dependent on cars, to the convenience of dormitory life. The university gave up its supervisory function during this period and the social experiences of men and women regained the similarity which had characterized them almost a century before.

In the same period following the war, other changes were occurring. The university experienced explosive growth in available resources, the physical plant, and the number of students admitted. In an affluent society, more women were able to seek and achieve admission as the university expanded. Women, as their numbers increased, became a visible presence on the campus.

The postwar years were marked also by the rapid movement of older women into the labor force: the working woman again became socially acceptable. Young women arrived at Cornell with stronger career orientation and sought more varied opportunities for training. They objected to restrictive admissions policies based on their sex. Other mature, highly educated women living in Ithaca sought work and found professional opportunity denied to them. The denial of economic equity to women became a strong motivating force for change.[10]

During the 1960s, isolated political activities coalesced into mass movements. Sentiment against the war in Vietnam was intense and disruptive at Cornell, and increasing political activism among black students contributed to the mounting turmoil. The basic assumptions and the very structure of the university were severely threatened by the disorder of students. Female activists soon learned that sex, not ability, determined their role in the political movements. Women were making coffee, not policy; they were secretaries, not leaders; and they were often valued most highly for their sexual attributes.

The 1960s were years of ferment and turbulence, of strong emphasis on individual freedom and intense testing of rigid institutions. In this social climate, not unlike that of the early nineteenth century in central New York which had given rise to the original drive for sexual equality, women were once again aware of their status as a minority, deprived of economic, political, and social opportunity, because of their sex. Strong-minded women again spoke out to demand equality and a wider sphere for women. Between 1967 and 1970, seven new women's organizations were formed on the Cornell campus.[11] Some women were

Militant women students march out the main entrance of Willard Straight Hall in 1970 to protest sex discrimination in the university's health care system. (Cornell University, Office of Public Information.)

dedicated to radical reform while others organized the Professional Skills Roster to identify employment opportunities.

The catalyst for this burgeoning discontent was Sheila Tobias, who came to the university in 1968 seeking an administrative position. The typing test to which she was subjected while male applicants were given aptitude tests served to convert her into an active feminist. Tobias subsequently became the assistant to the Vice President for

Academic Affairs and more important, the determined organizer of diverse women with common concerns.

The informal dialogue on the status of women received fresh impetus from the appearances on campus of articulate activists Kate Millet and Betty Friedan. In the course of the discussions, another woman became involved. Margaret Feldman, the wife of a Cornell professor and a member of the faculty of nearby Ithaca College, had long been concerned with the special problems of women as a result of her personal experience and her professional interest in psychology. She used a new word to describe the social constraints that affect women. She added the word "sexism" to the feminists' lexicon.

Three days in January 1969 were milestones in the history of women at Cornell. At this time, the Cornell Conference on Women, organized by Sheila Tobias and a committee of thirty women from all segments of the community, was held. This meeting was significant for several reasons. First, the 2,000 participants represented a broad spectrum from faculty wives to radical male students. By sharing their concerns, they promoted widespread consciousness raising. Second, although no specific objectives were established or policy agreements reached, the conference was important as a vehicle for public expression of massive dissatisfaction with the rigidity of sex roles and the male orientation of social institutions. The discussion illuminated the psychological, social, educational, and political barriers that have tended to prevent women from realizing Cornell's promise of diversity in human development. Third, this meeting was one of the first conferences held in the United States during the 1960s to define the dimensions of sexism within the academic framework.

The success of this conference demonstrated that there was intense interest in women's issues. At the same time, a group of students who had organized a seminar on racism the previous semester decided to develop a seminar on women in the spring of 1969. Their student-taught course, arranged under the auspices of the College of Home Economics and sponsored by Professor Harold Feldman, was the first course on women offered at Cornell. In the spring semester of 1970 an interdisciplinary course, "The Evolution of the Female Personality: History and Prospects," one of the first to be offered for credit by a major university, attracted over two hundred students. As a result of the conference and the development of an early credit course in women's studies, Cornell University stood once again in the forefront of the feminist movement, as it had a century before.

With the university in the process of rebuilding a campus community which had been shaken by dissension in the late 1960s and with the momentum for change established, there was additional impetus for reform from the expanding feminist movement outside the campus and from federal affirmative action legislation. [12] Between 1970 and 1976, policies and programs were revised to provide more extensive opportunities for women.

After some experimental courses were offered through a Female Studies Program, the Women's Studies Program was formally established in 1972 in the College of Arts and Sciences to promote teaching and research on the status of women. By 1975, seventy-five courses had been offered to provide a multidisciplinary perspective on women and over 1,600 students had been involved, one-fifth of whom were men. [13] Under the direction of Jennie T. Farley, the program has become an important center for women on the campus, a source of employment for women lecturers who are committed role models for students, and it has provided effective outreach programs for the community and Cornell alumnae. Graduate students can now develop a minor field in Women's Studies. With limited funding, the Women's Studies Program has become a model for other colleges and universities and, most important, is a vital source of support for Cornell women in a male-oriented institution.

To compensate for the lack of women in the administra-

Jennie T. Farley '54 received her Ph.D. in 1970, following her marriage and the birth of three children. From 1972 to 1976, she was assistant professor in the School of Industrial and Labor Relations and Director of the Women's Studies Program. Under her leadership, this innovative venture grew into a strong interdisciplinary program of scholarly inquiry into the place of women in society. The academic courses, seminars, and special projects provided through the Women's Studies Program supplement and enrich the traditional curriculum. (Cornell University, Office of Public Information.)

tion and to conduct research on the status of women, the Provost's Advisory Committee on the Status of Women, composed of women faculty, students, and employees, was appointed in 1971–1972. This group has repeatedly urged the appointment of women to the faculty and administration, as well as the revision of employment policies and practices. In January 1972, the Board of Trustees formed a committee which was charged to study the status of women faculty, students, and employees and to make recommendations for improvement. The public hearings held by this group gave added legitimacy to the claims of sex bias, and the final report, issued in 1974, clarified in statistical terms for the first time the low status of women as workers and as students at Cornell. For example, a thorough study demonstrated that women constituted only 7.5 percent of the Cornell faculty in 1973, with 3 percent serving as full professors. Of this limited number, over half of the women faculty were concentrated in the College of Human Ecology.[14] The Committee on the Status of Women presented specific recommendations for reform of all practices that militated against the full development and employment of women. Their report was the final step in the definition of problems that had constrained women at Cornell for many years.

Since 1970, changes have been made to improve the position of women. The university's policy statement on equal opportunity was amended to include sex among the proscribed criteria with regard to admission to the university. The use of gender-free nouns and pronouns is encouraged in all publications. New employment procedures have been instituted, such as including more women on search committees and publishing available job openings. Part-time positions on the faculty have been provided, with benefits and access to tenure available. Antinepotism policies were gradually abolished and by 1976 the faculty included twenty-six couples.[15] Women are now faculty members in units such as the History Department and the Law School, which previously employed only males.

As some women gained a foothold on the academic career ladder, others achieved the coveted rank of full professor in units outside the College of Human Ecology. In the College of Arts and Sciences, Eleanor Gibson after sixteen years as a research associate, became professor of psychology in 1965, and in 1972 was chosen to hold an endowed chair at Cornell, the first woman selected for such a position. It is one of the ironies of history that this achievement for women occurred in the name of one of the most disapproving participants in the drama of coeducation at Cornell, for Gibson became the Susan Linn Sage Professor of Psychology. Another woman, who had promoted the cause of women faculty for many years with limited success, took personal action to counter the scarcity of women professors. Mary Donlon, now Mrs. Alger, endowed a professorship specifically for a woman and this chair is held by Eleanor H. Jorden, professor of linguistics.

Women began to appear as professors and also in new roles as university administrators. In 1975, June M. Fessenden-Raden was appointed Vice Provost, the first woman to hold such a high administrative position. In 1976, Constance E. Cook was selected for the newly created post of Vice President for Land Grant Affairs, another significant achievement for her, for women, and for the university.

As women moved vertically in the university hierarchy, they also moved horizontally into other new positions, some functioning as sex counselors and career counselors, closely attuned to the needs of women. In the Office of University Development, one women supervises corporate and business affairs and another directs relations with foundations.

There were some triumphs for women and there was some progress for them by 1975, but in terms of overall improvement in employment opportunity, the results were disappointing. There were several reasons for this discouraging situation. The federal government, having enacted affirmative action legislation in recent years, failed to exercise strong leadership in its implementation. Some people in Ithaca resented federal intervention in what they considered university responsibilities. Affirmative action programs on this complex campus were difficult to manage and did not produce many positive results. President Dale R. Corson recommended the formation of the Affirmative Ac-

Constance E. Cook '41, LL.B. '43, is the first woman and first Cornell alumna to serve in the highest level of university administration. Her varied experiences as an attorney, a university trustee, and a member of the New York State Assembly are invaluable in her new position as Vice President for Land Grant Affairs. Cook is married and the mother of two. (Cornell University, Photographic Services.)

tion Advisory Board to analyze the current status of women and minorities and to propose more effective procedures.

In addition, the Cornell Women's Caucus was organized by faculty and staff members to monitor the progress of women, both academic and nonacademic. This group found that women continue to be overrepresented in all the lowest levels of employment and underutilized at the highest levels. While the number of women faculty has increased by 1 percent in the past five years, about half of these women are in the College of Human Ecology and some units still have no women faculty. Furthermore, the caucus has shown that the ratio of net increase of men to women on the Cornell faculty is two to one. A numerical comparison was made of the women employed in academic and nonacademic positions at Cornell and at forty other major universities, and a similar comparison was made with faculties at Dartmouth, Princeton, and Yale, all of which have recently become coeducational. These comparisons suggest that Cornell is lagging behind other institutions in employing women as faculty and staff. [16]

Although women have made only limited progress in achieving faculty rank, their representation on the Board of Trustees is improving. In contrast to a historical pattern of two or three women at a time on the board, in 1976 ten women were members out of a total membership of sixty-two. [17] Through the efforts of these women, the Cornell Board of Trustees sponsored a conference in October 1976 for women trustees and administrators of Ivy League institutions and the Massachusetts Institute of Technology, the first such meeting specifically for women involved in university governance. Named to honor the many years of service that Mary Donlon Alger had given as Cornell trustee, this meeting was convened to consider ways in which women in policy-making positions could function more effectively and improve the status of women in their institutions. Once again, those at Cornell University provided leadership for women in the academic community.

Many long-established constraints on the lives of women students have been removed and as a result the experiences of women at Cornell are more like those of men. With the removal of the dormitory residence requirement, all dormitories have become coeducational except one, which is restricted to women by the terms of its endowment. The abolition of the female bed quota and more receptive attitudes among administrators have increased the opportunity for women to enter formerly male-only schools. There have been dramatic changes in enrollment patterns between 1970 and 1976. For example, the number of women in the College of Agriculture has grown from 19 to 42 percent of the enrollment; in Business and Public Administration, from 3 to 19 percent; in the College of Engineering, from 2 to 12 percent; in Hotel Administration, from 10 to 23 percent; in Industrial and Labor Relations, from 15 to 34 percent; in Law, from 7 to 25 percent; and in Veterinary Medicine, from 4 to 34 percent. In response to pressure from women, the College of

Mary Smith, '69, D.V.M. '72, provides professional health care for large animals in the Ithaca area. At the college ambulatory clinic, she treats horses, sheep, and swine, and is shown checking a calf recovering from pneumonia. (Cornell University, Office of Public Information.)

Jamie Sylvester '73 stood first in her class in chemical engineering, and she was the first Cornell woman to be awarded a national scholarship by the Society of Women Engineers. In 1973 the Cornell chapter of this national professional organization was formally recognized, had thirty undergraduate women as charter members, and proposed to function as a support group for women engineers. (Cornell University, Office of Public Information.)

Arts and Sciences decided in 1970 to strive toward a goal of equal admissions for both sexes, with some allowances made for flexibility and individual differences. In 1976, 47 percent of those admitted to this college were women.[18]

The composition of the student body in the College of Home Economics is also different. Since 1970, the number of male undergraduates has risen from 3 to 12 percent.[19] This shift is one of many changes which resulted from a self-study conducted by the college faculty and staff. A new name, the College of Human Ecology, was adopted in 1969 and reflects changing goals and priorities in this unit. Purely domestic concerns have been supplanted by a broader perspective on the interrelationships between family, community, and society; the focus is no longer confined to rural life but includes urban areas as well; and the college aims to prepare its students for professional work in agencies involved in human service.

Other transformations have occurred on the Cornell campus in the changing social climate of the 1970s. Student life is less structured and formal, priorities are different, and many of the past constraints on women's experiences are no longer functional or acceptable. Women have been elected to high positions in student organizations, they are selected for awards presented at graduation to outstanding seniors, are admitted to the band, and can even be cheerleaders. Throughout the 1960s, male and female class organizations merged into single units, alumni classes joined together, some alumni clubs have become integrated, and eventually the Federation of Cornell Men's Clubs and the Federation of Cornell Women's Clubs united into a single organization. After more than eighty years of segregation, the senior male honorary societies voted to admit women and the women's honorary societies voted to admit men. After ninety years of military training at Cornell, women are now enrolled in the ROTC program, have been commissioned as officers at graduation, and some are financing their education by means of ROTC scholarships. Almost a century after the original men's musical group voted specifically to exclude women from membership, the Cornell Men's Glee Club voted to admit women who sing tenor or bass, although none has as yet been found.

One of the most significant changes for women has occurred in the area of athletics. For the first time in university history, a sports building for women was provided. Helen Newman Hall opened in the mid-1960s and immediately housed an extensive sports program. By 1976 there were more than sixteen teams in intercollegiate competition in such sports as ice hockey, crew, fencing, polo, track, tennis, and gymnastics.

Over one hundred years after it was first proposed by Andrew D. White in the 1866 Plan of Organization for Cornell University, the original goal, the encouragement of human development in "its richest diversity," remains valid. Once again, efforts are under way to effect its implementation for women as well as for men. However, high hopes must be tempered by reality. As coeditor of the book *Academic Women on the Move,* Alice S. Rossi, a former research associate at Cornell and a prominent theorist of the feminist movement, includes her own view of the future in academic life. She speculates that prestigious institutions, in which political activism and student unrest encouraged the early formation of women's groups demanding equity in the 1960s, may not be the first to rectify discriminatory practices. Institutions similar to Cornell, she suggests, spawned the rebirth of feminism on the college campus because the problems of sex discrimination were most severe. These institutions will also resist reform because of their deeply imbedded traditions of male superiority.[20]

Furthermore, it became evident in the 1970s that colleges and universities must contend with socio-economic trends which imply dwindling financial resources, shrinking enrollments, and declining need for faculty and staff. In the no-growth climate of the future, the options for women and men will tend to be limited by economic stringency, in contrast to those opened by the affluence of the recent past.

The interplay of ideological and economic determinants has shaped the evolution of coeducation. Contemporary economic pressures may diminish recent gains for women unless there is intensified ideological commitment to diversity in human development, the visionary concept which originally motivated Ezra Cornell, Andrew D. White, and others.

LaVerne Rolle '74 is a graduate of the New York State School of Industrial and Labor Relations. In recognition of her leadership in student activities and her community service, Rolle was selected by the Federation of Cornell Clubs as an outstanding senior of the Class of 1974. For the first time in the twenty-seven-year history of this award, a woman and a man were equally honored. (Cornell University, Office of Public Information.)

When the strong-minded women of Sage College were struggling to preserve their personal freedom, Professor Simon H. Gage and his wife Susanna attempted to offer them encouragement. In 1884, the Gages wrote, "Although the results may seem to be long in coming to fruition, yet doubtless there will come a time when in matters of education and general justice, there will be human beings, and not men and women."[21] Such a time will come only if there is steadfast commitment and constant encouragement directed to the similarities between the sexes, rather than the differences.

Appendix 1:
Survey of Alumnae

In an effort to ascertain the views of some alumnae, a search was made in 1972 of the monthly issues of the *Cornell Alumni News*, 1969–1972. In this magazine, each class publishes a column of news about members, compiled from letters from individuals who report on their own or friends' activities. This source of information provided the most efficient means of identification but it is limited in scope. The news items come from a self-selected group of people who have positive feelings toward the university. Others less satisfied with their educational experience do not generally maintain this contact, a factor which has little correlation with their later achievements.

Since the survey was originally undertaken to convince the skeptical student that "worthwhile" alumnae do exist, I selected sixty-one women who appeared in these news items not to have conformed to the usual pattern of marriage and motherhood. The basic criterion of selection was a commitment to an occupation considered unusual for women or the combination of a serious commitment outside the home with family responsibilities.

The purpose of the survey, to identify exceptional women, also served to limit the age range of the respondents. Women were included from the Class of 1912 to the Class of 1962, but the majority had graduated in the 1940s and 1950s. They were at this time past the primary demands of motherhood, well established in their life-styles, and so were more likely to be reporting serious interests beyond the family.

Forty-three women from a broad geographic area responded to the survey. One lived in a Manhattan brownstone house, another on a ranch in Montana, while a third lived in Honolulu, Hawaii. Marital status could not be a specific criterion of selection under the circumstances, but most respondents proved to be married with husbands present, with approximately 25 percent single, widowed, or divorced.

The pattern of combining education and marriage varied widely. One woman met her future husband during her first week as a Cornell freshman and left school at the end of that year to marry. After twenty years, four children, and travels around the world in connection with her husband's career, she returned to college to complete the requirements for a bachelor's degree. Another, a grandmother, undertook a strenuous graduate program following the death of her husband, earned a master's degree when she was over forty-five, and now enjoys professional success as a social worker.

These women represent a broad spectrum of talent and active involvement. There is a chemical engineer, a language teacher, an architect, a veterinarian, and a chemist. One woman, an ordained minister, was unable to obtain employment in this role many years ago because of her sex and so developed an unusually productive career as a teacher, author, and lecturer. Several others were successful authors, with their works ranging from novels and nonfiction to science fiction. Two women have held high positions in the federal government, one has served in a state legislature, and one was elected to a city council. While one was the first woman to achieve faculty status at a certain law school, another had accomplished the same feat at a particular medical school. Many Cornell women, as lawyers, economists, psychologists, and sociologists have committed themselves to enlarging the sphere of women through their research, their teaching, and their efforts to challenge the contemporary barriers to women. As informed volunteers, others were striving to effect change in the environment, the legal system, and in education. Many reported academic honors as undergraduates and in later life, a variety of professional and civic achievements.

The survey was not meant to obtain a scientific sampling, but rather to gather information and observations from a limited, atypical group of Cornell alumnae. Although the women were similar in their divergence from the assumed female role, their opinions varied in emphasis and concern. In addition to basic biographical data, responses to the following questions were solicited. Included are selected answers which are representative of the total received.

What have proven to be the most relevant aspects of your Cornell education?

Its diversity. Every single course I took at Cornell that diverged from standard and major subjects has been professionally valuable, from paleontology to floriculture, from history of architecture to freehand drawing. I regret to this day that I gave in to my English professor advisor's refusal to let me take farm management, cattle-judging, and bee-keeping. The bee-keeping is the only thing I haven't needed so far. When I took all that drama just for fun, I had no idea I'd be paying my taxes as a drama critic some day, and when I took city planning, I didn't know I'd be on a planning team. It was all so useful because it was so varied.

Since my entire professional education was at Cornell, it has had a profound effect on my life, in that most of the technical basis for my life work was acquired there. It was a good basis and served me well.

When I got into college, my freshman Zoology instructor and everyone in the department was so excited and so enthusiastic about what they were doing, they made it all so interesting. My instructor would get all excited and say "Hey, come see what Sue's got in her microscope." There was real enthusiasm. It was that kind of experience that made me know that I wanted to go on and major in Zoology.

The fact that I had it. Although I did not "use" my knowledge professionally for twenty years, it was there and reflected my range of interests and knowledge about all kinds of things. It opened the door to my employment as a social worker using my formal educational background, then later to graduate school. The diversity of courses was important. I can hold my own in almost any kind of discussion.

The bigness of the place had a lot to do with my being able to attempt reasonably big things. In the Women's Athletic Association, for instance, we were trying to run an athletic program for all those women and we didn't have much to work with, but we just went ahead and did the best we could. On the Women's Judiciary Board, we had in our hands the decision of whether a girl stayed or left or whether she could be penalized. I think we had great responsibilities. The kinds of things we dealt with, mostly, were girls who stayed out too late, occasionally a girl who would go to a boy's apartment. At that time, I think the seriousness of it was not anything intrinsic to the situation but the fact that a girl could be sent home. No girl could be sent home without a lot of thought.

The diversity of it and the learning to cope with people, schedules, pressure, and a variety of forms of information and data. I combined a major in physics with a near-major in extra-curricular activities (an editor of the *Cornell Daily Sun*, etc.) I learned as much from one as from the other and have never regretted the time and effort spent on either, although I have since digressed a long way from being a physicist.

I got a good traditional undergraduate education in English literature, which I knew I wanted, and no idea at all how to make a living. I learned that I knew nothing about "life" because I didn't write about rape, barroom brawls, murdering animals, etc. so I decided, in part because of this, to write science fiction. I loved the countryside around Cornell and learned a great deal from it. I learned that people would read what I wrote and the pleasure and joy I got from that was very important (a kind of support Yale denied me, mostly because I wrote rotten plays). Cornell is ideal for someone like me, who knew exactly what she wanted.

The excellence of the child development program at Cornell. My instructors were inspiring and demanded a lot of me, contrary to the stereotype of home economics training. I had no difficulty being accepted into traditional psychology graduate programs and no problem competing with graduate students who had gone the Arts and Sciences undergraduate route. Had this "home ec" major occurred at another school, I am certain it would have been held against me.

How did the coeducational experience affect your life?

My father was Class of 1913 and he was horrified about my coming to Cornell. I had applied on my own. When I was accepted, my father said he could never go back and face his friends, now that his daughter was a coed. When he was here, they (the coeds) were dirt under their feet. The men in his fraternity were fined for even speaking to a coed and they had their fraternity pins taken away if they dated a coed. And yet, when I was here, I couldn't believe it, there was no problem in any way. No, I never felt put down because I was a coed, except in a joking sort of way. Except for the old routine of dating somebody and then having them invite an import to houseparty.

I learned never to allow the presence of men to interfere with my thought processes or the expression of my ideas.

The ratio was not good and made many false situations. I cannot imagine non-coeducational classes. I suppose the coed classes made me expect to be considered equal in discussions and conversations since then. This hasn't always happened. With intimate friends, this is not so, because we sort of look beyond the male-female role to each as individuals but in larger circles, I do get the feeling that my opinions are not sought or as well regarded. I really think it is the business of role expectations and at Cornell, there was more community of expectations.

I've always been in coed situations and enjoy the blend of competition and flirtation that usually evolves. The stylistic differences between the sexes adds in my experience to awareness and productivity, at least in my field.

With the other girls of my class, I resented having so many of the men regard us as interlopers in their rightful domain.

I had a very good time socially at Cornell and the lives of my close friends served as negative models, much the same as my mother's life did. I did not want to become what they were becoming. They were there to find a man, with money preferably, and to establish comfortable homes, and have babies as soon as possible. The men, with few exceptions, were just as materialistic and unconcerned about societal problems. Even the guy I was pinned to for a long time who did go on and get a graduate degree, told me he couldn't let me do that sort of thing. But you have to remember that one of the reasons I went to college was to have a good time and you could, with these kinds of people in that sheltered, isolated, unreal environment. Cornell lived up to its reputation as a party school, which was one reason I was there.

I guess I loved my years there. It's not that they were "the best years of my life" in the old alumnus sense. I was 16, unhappy and limited at home. I had never been away. I had never known a boy, since I had always gone to girls' schools. I had no social life. At Cornell, I found boys who were friends and boys who became lovers—that is, in the old sense, no real sex. I found girls who were friends, my youth. I don't think I would have emerged from adolescence or been able to work in a largely male newspaper setting without the coeducational experience I had at Cornell.

I liked the ratio. It never occurred to me that I couldn't do anything a man could do while I was at Cornell. The thing I remember about social life was the big difference between the coeds and the imports at parties, when they came for weekends. They had such a different attitude towards men. We were much more matter-of-fact. My sister at Wellesley didn't have a date for an evening the way we did. She always had a date for a weekend and very often, she'd say that she never wanted to see that guy again.

I always felt the rules we had for coeds were a good thing and I'm not sure I agree with the newer freedoms of coed groups.

What have been the most important factors which determined your choice of activities since college?

It was a combination of self-determination and happenstance. Self-determination was the return to graduate school and the working world after being a housewife. Happenstance was the move of my husband and family to Washington, and the job opportunities that opened. Of great importance has been the willingness of my family, particularly my husband, to share household tasks and put up with uncertain hours.

My training at Cornell led me first into teaching. The Vietnam War, which I opposed, prompted my interest in politics. That interest led me to active participation in campaigns for anti-war candidates and on to my present position in local government. My work with the local League of Women Voters has been extremely valuable in that it developed understanding of the community and state, and was a training ground on political issues.

The movements of my husband have been very important. It is only recently that we have begun to think of our careers as co-equal. The rest of it has been a matter of "hanging in there," with a lot of hard work and a lot of luck.

Chance, necessity, cowardice, opportunity, my husband's choice of profession, my own skill at writing, I suppose, and my great good luck at selling a story which finally, at nearly fifty, led to my first published novel. I should have started at twenty. Really, I see now the current notions of what women's role should be. So I retreated home in the fifties because I thought I should be a good wife and mother: my husband incidentally didn't agree at all. I sat on myself earlier for similar reasons. I am still too brainwashed to take advantage of my opportunities.

I ran the United Appeal for our city the year Susie was in kindergarten a half day. I spent hours on the telephone. I just invested hours of time and also exhausted my family's patience with all that telephoning. One day, my husband came home and said "You're getting the weeds out of your garden but you've got weeds growing in your mind. There are a lot of people who could be running the United Appeal. You've got a good mind and you

ought to be using it for something that might not be done otherwise."

When I got into volunteer work, my husband resented it. When
I got involved in developing a new organization in our town, he
resented it. I tried to compensate, but I finally got to the point
where I have to be me. You have to be an individual. That doesn't
mean you can't be devoted to each other but you have to have a
sense of being other. Maybe a college education is bad?

My intelligence and high motive to achieve, plus my disdain for
materialism. Also, I enjoy working hard.

Hard, hard to say. At the time, I thought it was my own inclina-
tion that was prompting me to work half-time or full-time, pursue
various volunteer activities, and so forth. Now, in reflecting on it,
I see that, of course, I was constrained by my husband's career and
the places his work took him.

I've tried to tailor my activities and schedule to meet the needs
of my children. From the birth of the first child until the youngest
entered first grade, I did very little work away from home.
I've had some great opportunities. In India, I had a chance to
help in a study of a yoga's heart rhythms. In Brazil, I was able to
do research on pedestrian fatalities.
I have given up most of my volunteer work because I feel I am
most productive doing work for which I have some unique training. My priorities outside the home are largely determined by trying to figure out what will be of greatest benefit to society. I am
fortunate to work in a field where I can literally save lives, but that
opportunity imposes the burden of trying to figure out "What is
important, and is not likely to be done unless I do it?"

Volunteer work was fine for a while but professional status
seems to give one more authority and freedom to be creative.

What have been your sources of greatest satisfaction?
My greatest satisfactions are my husband and my children. I
thoroughly enjoy all my other activities and love being just myself

doing something like teaching, but there is no doubt that the family is my greatest satisfaction and a tremendous one.

My work has been a great satisfaction to me. I cannot imagine my life without it, anymore than I can imagine my life without the family experiences we have shared. Now that the children are older, my work has even greater meaning for me.

Success and recognition as a good teacher have been dividends which a good education has paid and the fact that I can lay claim to them, as well as to say that I have managed to produce three very satisfactory sons and that my husband has been able to look upon me as a homemaker, as well as a financial asset, gives me satisfaction.

I think working is so much more fun than playing and so much more interesting. The person who does it ends up having a lot more fun. The idea of sitting around playing bridge is just deadly.

Writing. Thinking. Being me-in-me, so to speak. Walking around and looking at things, mostly in the country. Teaching. Friends. Working in the women's movement which is something I've gotten into only lately but has become extremely important to me. Real work and real love, as Virginia Woolf says—those two categories cover everything. In the past few years, I've made real women friends for the first time and these friendships have become a real source of enormous support and help.

The enormous personal satisfaction of working hard at my profession and making a contribution; the gratification of family life; the experience of living in cultures other than my own; the opportunity to have diverse, intense, satisfying friendships.
It hasn't all been roses. There've been times when I've had to reassess over and over how much it is worth to me to be married and to be a parent.

What advice would you give to a woman entering Cornell?
I would warn her that Cornell is a large school in which she must be prepared to work independently and to seek her own

friends and life-style. I don't think Cornell provides many sup-
ports for the student, male or female, who is unsure of himself.
But it offers a real intellectual challenge to the student who is self-
motivated and self-directed.

A woman entering Cornell today should come with some knowledge of the demands that coeducational living will place upon her.

To affirmatively seek out opportunities to work with peer groups
and faculty to establish full equality for men and women in all
aspects of university life.

Use the opportunity to explore any and all fields which interest
you. This is the one time in your life when you can do it easily.
Don't be channeled into courses of study or activities which are
"appropriate." The need to prepare oneself with a background
specific for a given career, with a few exceptions such as medicine
or law, seems unreal to me. I know of few jobs which my peers are
doing which can't be learned on the job by someone of intelligence
and energy. Think of yourself first and your individuality. Don't
assume your future is inextricable from a husband and family. If
that woman shares my concerns about the liberation of minorities
and women, I would also advise her that she *can* make a difference. Too many people assume that little can be done and consequently never try.

Be aware of the sexist bias present in almost all of the curriculum. Remember that Cornell has a peculiar isolation and a peculiar
malaise which many students find very unpleasant. There's something about the combination of climate, ivory-tower-ism, and conservatism that drives undergraduates into soul-crises, all about
The Meaning of It All. These seem not to occur in other places and
can be considered an effect of Lake Cayuga. Don't take them too
seriously. Resist the pressure to either marry or define yourself
vocationally. Most interesting and good people wallow about for
ten years after they graduate from college, trying first one thing
and then another. It's scary but it's not bad.

I would have had her take nontraditional-for-a-woman courses,
letting the history, creative writing, and art appreciation go for the
while. Science and math will add a freedom for future choices she

probably does not have when she arrives. I would say take classes from the greatest people around, take courses you are afraid of, work yourself to the limit intellectually. Struggle to free yourself from the patterns and people who have made you what you are. Make yourself over the way you choose.

Keep an open mind and heart. Appreciate your good luck in being given this opportunity.

What advice would you give a woman graduating from Cornell?

Plan a career but be sure to marry someone who sympathizes with your career goals. Life is also easier with just two children, preferably healthy. A big city is easier for a working mother than the suburbs.

Learn investing at an early age.

I would encourage graduate study. I would have her never accept a job which does not utilize her talents and college education. It is better to volunteer for no pay to do the thing you do best and which fulfills you most, than to compromise for security and status. If she weren't into Women's Lib, I'd recommend it. It represents a force no one should be deprived of, a source of personal growth that, throughout one's life, can teach new things about the self and others.

Use what you have learned and experienced to serve your society, to improve the position of woman in our society, and to do what is rewarding and gratifying to yourself. You can combine a family and a career if you and your husband consider it, work for it together, and plan to give sufficient time and thought to each aspect. Women with good minds and good education are needed as productive members of society, and as wives and mothers as well. Women are especially well suited to consider the problems of our society and push for constructive solutions to them. And besides, it's really lots of fun too.

Be aware of yourself as a person, not just a woman. You are part of the human race. Accept and choose the role you can play in the scheme of things, not singlehandedly to solve every problem in the world. Influence the sphere that is yours, widen it if you can, but never stop trying.

Every woman should have some seriously pursued interest which has nothing to do with her home and family.

Never base your actions on what you *think* other people may think. You can't possibly predict that for sure, so it is not a logical basis for judgment.

Don't subordinate your whole life to the career of a man, no matter who or what he is; no person is worth the using up of another person. Put him through medical school, if you have to, but keep your balance. Sacrifice hurts both the giver and the recipient in the long run.

The ability to organize time well is a thing I have found essential to me who must switch various roles (wife, mother, politician) on a regular basis.

Don't opt immediately for marriage. There's lots of growing and learning about oneself which is done in the few years after graduation. It's not wise to marry before undergoing that process. It's unlikely that it will be accomplished during marriage. Whatever you want, don't be discouraged from it and fight for it, if necessary.

Stay home with your children or work only part-time until they are in first grade. In the long run, it doesn't really hurt career or academic interests and it's important for children, mother, and family.

Never, never let an employer know you can type. Never, never use feminism as an excuse.

The most important decision you will make has to do with your own work, the way you will spend your life, how you will justify the air you breathe on this crowded planet. Don't marry in haste: don't, for heaven's sake, have a baby by mistake. Children are precious: rearing them is important work and hard. Parenthood, like marriage, shouldn't be entered into lightly.

Women have always been channeled into one kind of work, marriage and childrearing. Some young women and men are now saying that parenthood should be the responsibility of both and that women should have more chances to be in the outside world and men, more chance to be at home. They are experimenting with ways of sharing. One can be skeptical and say that it won't work or one can feel, as I do, that if enough people want to change society badly enough, they can and will.

I quote a black woman I met at a conference last month. She said, "We who are black and we who are women wear labels at this point in history." She's right, we do. We are thought of as black people or as women and not as individual human beings. She went on, "We who wear labels have to begin to think of ourselves as powerful. I am powerful. I can change things."

Appendix 2: Women's Self Government Association By-laws

1915

Full power to inflict penalties for disciplinary purposes has been delegated by the Faculty and by the Trustees of the University to the Committee on Student Affairs and to that Committee only. The Committee on Student Affairs has delegated to the Women's Self Government Association the authority to investigate charges of misconduct, other than fraud in examination, and to make recommendations concerning the same to the Committee on Student Affairs in accordance with the standing agreement between the Committee on Student Affairs and the Women's Self Government Association which is filed with the Secretary of the Association.

I.

A strict honor system shall prevail in every department of the University life.

Every undergraduate woman shall consider herself personally responsible for the maintenance of this system. Anyone observing an offence shall request the offender to report within 24 hours to the President of the Association. Cases for judgment shall be considered by the President of the Association in concurrence with the Advisor of Women who shall as they see fit refer it to the Student Government Association.

II.

While Day Students are not subject in general to the restrictions contained in the By-Laws, all undergraduate women students of the University are required to conform to the rule of the University which says: "A student is expected to show, both within and without the University, such respect for order, morality, personal honor, and the rights of others as is demanded of good citizens, gentlemen and ladies." One who fails to do this will be disciplined by the proper committee for infraction of this rule.

III.

All dormitories shall be closed at 10 P.M. except on Saturday, when the closing hour will be 10:30 P.M. All men callers are to be out of the house by the closing hour, and all undergraduate women shall be in unless registered. All residents of each house expecting to remain out after 10 P.M. are required to register their destination and approximate time of return. After 10 P.M. no resident shall be allowed to register unless special permission is granted by the Warden or someone designated by her. Women students, not resident in the dormitories or living at home are required to keep the same hours.

IV.

Going out of town or leaving the dormitory overnight is forbidden without the permission of the Warden. House parties come under this ruling and in all cases chaperonage must be passed upon by the Warden. Students leaving for vacation should notify the Warden.

V.

The members of the House Committee shall provide a proctoring system for the dormitory and under the direction of University officials shall take charge of the fire drills.

VI.

Proctors and sub-proctors must enforce the rules of quiet, i.e., Comparative quiet after 8 P.M.; absolute quiet from 10 P.M. to 7 A.M. (On Saturday nights quiet need not be maintained until 10:30 P.M.) On week-days pianos and victrolas may be used only between the following hours: 8 to 9 A.M., 12 to 2 P.M., 5 to 8 P.M.; Sundays 9 to 11 A.M., 1 to 3 P.M., 5 to 8 P.M.

VII.

All cases of illness must be immediately reported to the Warden. Students may have their social privileges curtailed at any time on the ground of ill health. The arrival of all guests must be reported at once to the Warden.

VIII.

The women of the University shall be in the dormitories at the closing time unless registered for one of the following:

1. Skating or tobogganing from which they shall return not later than 10:30.

2. The Library from which they shall return not later than 11.

3. Functions at which the University women are hostesses, from which they shall return not later than 12:30, all such functions closing not later than 12.

4. Other social functions and engagements, theatre, parties, etc., from which they shall return not later than 12.

5. Formal dances from which they shall return not later than 1:30.

6. The regularly scheduled functions of Junior and Senior weeks, the Military Hop and the Navy Ball are exceptions to this rule.

IX.

The Association assumes no responsibility for its members in regard to boating on Cayuga Lake. Permission is given only by special letter (to be filed with the Advisor of Women) from parent or guardian assuming all responsibility. Violation of this rule will be punished by University authority.

(a) A student who wishes to go upon the lake must consult the Warden of her hall or the person under whose care she is, informing her fully as to her arrangements and the probable time of return. All undergraduate women students must be in off the water by 8 P.M. unless special permission to do otherwise has been given by the Warden or the Executive Committee.

X.

On all occasions requiring chaperonage, the undergraduate women of the University must be under the care of chaperones approved by the Wardens.

(a) Undergraduate women of the University are not to appear at a hotel either with or without an escort except under the care of an approved chaperone.

(b) Women of the University are not to be driving after dark without an approved chaperone.

(c) Freshman going to and returning from dances, parties, theatre, etc., must always be chaperoned. Upper-classmen may serve as chaperones.

(d) Students other than freshman may attend church affairs, university functions and all out door sports, games and celebrations unchaperoned. Upperclassmen may act as chaperones for freshmen on these occasions.

(e) Freshmen may not walk after 8 o'clock with an escort. Groups of freshmen women without escorts may walk after 8 with an upperclass chaperone.

(f) A list of approved upperclass chaperones shall be posted by the Executive Committee.

XI.

No undergraduate woman of the University shall devote more than two nights a week to social diversion closing later than 11 o'clock.

(a) Sophomores shall not devote more than three nights a week to social diversions of any kind.

(b) Freshmen shall not devote more than two nights a week to social diversion of any kind.

(c) After the spring vacation freshmen have sophomore privileges and sophomores have upperclass privileges unless they are withdrawn by the Executive Committee for reason.

1952 Excerpts
1. *Class Standing*
2. *Late Nights*
   a. Living unit closing hours are:
      Monday through Thursday 12 midnight
      Friday   12:30 A.M.
      Saturday   1:30 A.M.
      Sunday   12 midnight
   b. A girl must be in her living unit by her class hours, which are:
      Freshmen   10:30 P.M.
      Sophomores 11:00 P.M.

> Juniors   12 midnight
> Seniors   12 midnight

c. Freshmen and sophomores are permitted to sign out until living unit closing hours two nights during a week. Such a sign out is called a "late night."

  1) A week begins on Monday.
  2) Registration of a caller in the living room after a student's class hours counts as one late night.

d. Senior permissions are granted to all women during examination week and official vacations.

e. Penalizations:

  1) One minute for each minute of lateness. If 15 or more minutes are acquired at one time, the case is reviewed by the House Committee.
  2) Two late nights taken away for using a third late night in one week, unless the third is a "special" late night (See Sect. 3)

3. *Special Permissions*

a. Social specials

  1) Freshmen and sophomores have 10 social "specials" a year, of which not more than five may be taken the first term. These specials may be used for additional late nights during a week when two late nights have already been taken.
  2) Juniors and seniors have two social specials a term for overnights in Ithaca (excluding sorority houses) during a week when a girl also wishes to take two late nights Friday and Saturday.
  3) Any requests for extending the number of specials under exceptional circumstances shall be addressed to the President of W S G A, for approval of the Executive Committee.
  4) A student may not take a social special on a night of penalization.

b. Activity, academic, and work specials

  1) Permission to participate in extra-curricular and academic activities beyond class hours is granted by the WSGA Special Permissions Board. Before calling a member of the Board, a girl should contact her VP for information.

2) A student must make arrangements for work specials at the office of the Dean of Women.

c. A 25-minute food leave is granted to all students between 11 P.M. and living unit closing hours. This food leave may be taken by a student who has been outside her living unit after 10:30 P.M.

1) A student may not take food leave on a night of penalization.

4. *Chaperone Rules*

a. No woman shall at any time go to a man's apartment or room, or to a fraternity house, except when:

1) She has specifically signed out to a party which has been registered at the Office of the Social Calendar. A list of registered parties is sent to each chaperone weekly by that office, and is posted in the living unit.

2) She has been given special permission to do so by her head resident for impromptu affairs and is accompanied by parents or chaperones, in which case she shall also sign out.

b. Penalization: review of the case by the Residence Council or Judiciary Committee.

5. *Signing Out on a White Slip*

a. A girl may not be out of her living unit after 10:30 P.M. unless she is signed out.

1) If a girl is in her living unit and wishes to sign out after 10:30 P.M., she may do so without penalization.

2) If a girl who has failed to sign out returns after 10:30 P.M. she may take one minute for each minute of lateness, or she may make out a signout slip in which case she takes a late night and is penalized for late registration. First and second late registrations—five minutes. Third and subsequent late registrations—10 minutes.

b. A girl must register a living room caller after 10:30 P.M. A caller may remain until the living unit closing hour (see Sec. 2-c-2).

c. A girl must sign out to a specific destination in order to facilitate immediate contact in case of emergency.

d. A girl leaving town for more than three hours during the day (including academic trips) must sign out as specifically as possible.

e. A girl who has boating privileges must sign out when using them.

f. If a girl has signed out to living unit closing hours or to her class hours, returns to the dormitory prior to the time to which she has signed out, and forgets to sign in, she shall receive five minutes penalty. This does not apply when a girl has signed out on a white slip for the daytime or early evening.

g. Penalization for failure to comply with Rules *d* and *e:* review of the case by the House Committee.

6. *Overnight Absences*
   a. General Instructions
      1) A girl must sign out *personally* with her head resident before leaving for an overnight absence.
      2) A girl must sign out to a specific destination. The University must know where she can be reached at all times.
   c. Overnight Absences at Houseparties
      1) A girl must sign out on a blue slip by 2 P.M. on the day of her departure. Penalization: first and second late registrations—five minutes; third and subsequent late registrations—10 minutes.
      2) Written permission from a parent or guardian sent directly to the head resident is necessary before registration for out-of-town houseparties will be approved.
      3) Registration for two-night houseparties in town shall count as two social late nights. Registration for two-night houseparties out of town shall count as one social late night.
      4) In signing out for a houseparty a girl shall put the name of her date on the back of her sign-out slip. Penalization for failure to do so—five minutes.
      5) A girl may sign out until one-half hour beyond the official registration of a houseparty in town.
   e. Overnight Absences Out of Town
      1) A girl must sign out on a pink slip by 2:00 P.M. of the day of departure. Penalization: first and second late registrations—five minutes; third and subsequent late registrations—10 minutes.

2) Written permission from the parent or guardian sent directly to the head resident is necessary before registration for any overnight out-of-town absence (except when visiting the home of parents or guardian) will be approved.

   a) Permission of the parent or guardian is not required of a married girl living in University living units for an out-of-town absence, since she is no longer considered to be under parental jurisdiction.

   b) Blanket permission for out-of-town absences may be obtained from a girl's parent or guardian. A card provided for this purpose shall be sent upon request to the girl's parent or guardian by the head resident of the living unit, and must be returned directly to the head resident.

3) A head resident is expected to consult with the parents of a girl who wishes to leave Ithaca under questionable circumstances (e.g. weather, permission).

4) Women leaving Cornell by car for an overnight absence out of town must depart from Ithaca in time to reach their destination by twelve midnight, unless permission, sent directly to the head resident, is granted by the parents to drive at a later time.

5) Out-of-town absence, regardless of the number of days absent, will count as one late night out of the week the student returns if she returns any time after her class hours on Monday night. In case of emergencies, exceptions will be made by the President of WSGA or by the dormitory president.

7. *General Registration Rules*

   a. In any situation necessitating late return to a living unit after closing hours, a girl should notify her head resident by phone or wire. Special consideration for doing so will be given by the House Committee. This will save worry and effort on the part of the head resident and student University officers.

   b. A girl shall place her VP's initials in the upper right corner of both sign-out slips, and her class after her name (i.e. Fr, Soph, Jr, and Sr). If she is taking a "special," she shall indicate the type of "special" in the upper left corner of both slips. Repeated inaccuracy in signing out will result in review of the case by the House Committee after sufficient warning has been given by the girl's VP.

8. *Living Unit Regulations*
    a. Smoking and Drinking
        1) There shall be no smoking in the University Residential Halls except in the students' rooms. (Check any special arrangements for smoking elsewhere in the living unit with the dormitory president.)
        2) There shall be no drinking or possession of alcoholic beverages in any of the women's living units.
    b. Quiet Hours
        1) Quiet hours shall be maintained in the dormitories beginning at 8 P.M. on every night except Saturday when quiet hours shall begin at 10:30 P.M. and extend until 12 noon each day. Quiet also shall be maintained from 2 to 5 P.M. each day except Saturday. Any dorm may, if necessary, modify the above plan as the House Committee sees fit.
    d. Registration of Parties in the Living Units
        1) All parties, dances, etc. shall be registered in the Office of the Social Calendar by the preceding Wednesday at 3 P.M. A girl wishing to give a party should contact her social chairman about arrangements.
        2) An organization or group of students planning a large picnic shall register it so that it can be held indoors in case of rain. Any organized group giving a picnic lasting later than 10:30 P.M. shall have such a picnic registered. A girl attending the picnic shall sign out to it.
    e. A girl entering a living unit after 10:30 P.M. shall stop at the desk and give her name and living unit. Penalization for failure to do so—five minutes.

9. *University Ruling on Boating*

10. *WSGA Meetings*
    a. Members may not be excused from class meetings except for illness, two prelims, a prelim and a paper, or two papers due the following day. Penalization, 10 minutes.
    b. Excuses from corridor or house meetings are granted at the

discretion of the V P or House President respectively. Penalization for unexcused absence, 5 minutes.

c. Excuses from district or dorm meetings are granted by the V P or dormitory president respectively. Penalization for unexcused absence, 5 minutes.

11. *Penalizations*

d. Range of Penalizations

1) Reprimand

2) Loss of Friday or Saturday late nights (meaning a girl must be in her living unit by 10:30 P.M. on the night or nights of penalization).

3) Freshman rules: a girl must be in her living unit by 10:30 P.M. every night of the week or weeks in which she is penalized. The penalization of signing in at the desk between 10:20 and 10:30 P.M. every night may also be added.

4) Suspension may be recommended by the WSGA Judiciary Committee, subject to review by the Faculty Committee on Student Conduct.

5) Expulsion may be recommended by the WSGA Judiciary Committee, subject to review by the Faculty Committee on Student Conduct.

Notes

Items located in the Department of Manuscripts and University Archives, Cornell University Libraries are identified by the abbreviation DMUA.

Preface

1. Thomas Woody, *A History of Women's Education in the United States* (New York, 1929), p. 258; Mabel Newcomer, *A Century of Higher Education for American Women* (New York, 1959), p. 153.

2. Liva Baker, "The 'Seven Sisters' Are Celebrating Their Centenaries," *Smithsonian Magazine*, Feb. 1974, p. 84.

3. Changes in the educational and career orientation of women are discussed in the following books: William L. O'Neill, *Everyone Was Brave: A History of Feminism in America* (Chicago, 1969); William H. Chafe, *The American Woman: Her Changing Social, Economic, and Political Roles, 1920–1970* (New York, 1972); and Judith Hole and Ellen Levine, *Rebirth of Feminism* (New York, 1971). Statistical documentation can be found in Women's Bureau, Department of Labor, *Trends in Educational Attainment of Women* (Washington, D.C., Oct. 1969).

4. Mary S. Jaffe to Charlotte Conable, 18 Feb. 1977.

Prologue

1. *New York Herald Tribune*, 4 Dec. 1935, quoted in *Bryn Mawr Alumnae Bulletin*, Jan. 1936, p. 20.

2. *Reports of Cases Argued and Determined in the Supreme Court of*

the State of Wisconsin, XXXIX (Chicago, 1876), 245, quoted in Robert W. Smuts, *Women and Work in America* (New York, 1971), p. 110.

3. Jean Jacques Rousseau, *Emile*, trans. Barbara Foxley (London, 1911), p. 328.

4. Daniel Defoe, *Essays on Projects*, quoted in Mabel Newcomer, *A Century of Higher Education for American Women* (New York, 1959), p. 32.

5. Judith Sargent Murray, "On the Equality of the Sexes (1790)," quoted in *Up from the Pedestal*, ed. Aileen Kraditor (Chicago, 1968), p. 32.

6. Mary Wollstonecraft, *The Vindication of the Rights of Women* (1792: rpt. New York, 1967), pp. 247–250.

Chapter 1. New York: The Frontier of Ideas.

1. Samuel Eliot Morrison, *The Oxford History of the American People* (New York, 1965), II, 234.

2. *Ibid.*, p. 237.

3. Harry G. Good, *A History of American Education* (New York, 1968), p. 113.

4. Edward T. James and Janet Wilson James, eds., *Notable American Women: A Biographical Dictionary* (Cambridge, Mass., 1971), III, 610–613. Hereinafter cited as *NAW*.

5. Whitney R. Cross, *The Burned-Over District: The Social and Intellectual History of Enthusiastic Religion in Western New York, 1800–1850* (Ithaca, N.Y., 1950).

6. Ralph V. Harlow, *Gerrit Smith: Philanthropist and Reformer* (New York, 1972), is an excellent source of information on this colorful figure.

7. Biographical data on Stanton is found in sources listed in Bibliography and also in *NAW*, III, 342–347. A study was made by the author, "Elizabeth Cady Stanton 1815–1902: Portrait of a New Yorker" (term project, Women's Studies 221, George Washington University, Spring 1973).

8. Harriot S. Blatch and Theodore Stanton, eds., *Elizabeth Cady Stanton as Revealed in Her Letters, Diary, and Reminiscences* (New York, 1922), I, 142.

9. Blatch and Stanton, II, 21.

10. *NAW*, I, 161–165.

11. *NAW*, I, 654–655.

12. *NAW*, I, 497–499.

13. Blatch and Stanton, II, 19–20.

14. *NAW*, I, 179–181.

15. *NAW*, II, 540–541.

16. *NAW*, I, 158–161.

17. Alma Lutz, *Susan B. Anthony: Rebel, Crusader, Humanitarian* (Boston, 1959); *NAW*, I, 51–57.

18. Elizabeth Stanton to Susan Anthony, 2 April 1852, quoted in Elizabeth Cady Stanton, *Eighty Years and More: Reminiscences 1815–1897* (1898; rpt. New York, 1971), p. x.

19. People's College Association, Resolution, 20 Aug. 1851, quoted in Waterman T. Hewett, *Cornell University: A History* (New York, 1905), I, 45.

20. Susan Anthony to Harrison Howard, 15 Sept. 1852, People's College Collection, DMUA.

21. Harrison Howard, "Sketch of the Origin of the Mechanics Mutual Protective Organization and the Establishment of the People's College" (unpublished manuscript, 1886), pp. 37–38, People's College Collection, DMUA.

22. "Women's Rights in the Legislature," *Albany Register*, 7 March 1854, quoted in Blatch and Stanton, I, 162–163.

23. Quoted in Lutz, *Susan B. Anthony*, p. 69.

24. John Stuart Mill and Harriet Taylor Mill, *Essays on Sex Equality*, ed. Alice S. Rossi (Chicago, 1970), pp. 112–113.

25. *NAW*, III, 532–533.

26. *NAW*, II, 229–231.

Chapter 2. The Founders: Male and Female

1. *Cornell Era*, 29 Sept. 1871, p. 27.

2. Dr. Elizabeth Blackwell to Ezra Cornell, 7 April 1865, Cornell papers, DMUA.

3. When the Cornell Medical College opened in 1898 and accepted women, Dr. Blackwell closed her Women's Medical College, which had operated successfully for thirty years, and the women students transferred to the Cornell Medical College.

4. See the "Mary Ann" letters, Cornell papers, DMUA.

5. Quoted in Hewett, *Cornell University*, I, 255–257.

6. The promised gift of the portrait is referred to both in *Autobiography of Andrew D. White* (1905; rpt. New York, 1932), I, 163–164, and *Memoir of S. J. May* (Boston, 1873), pp. 291–292. The condition that women be admitted to Cornell University appears only in the May volume. The portrait hangs in the Kirby Memorial Room of the Uris Library at Cornell and is reputedly one of the finest portraits in the university collection. Painted by Francis Alexander, it was commissioned in 1838 by the New England Anti-Slavery Society.

7. *Autobiography of Andrew D. White*, I, 398.

8. Memorial Booklet for Mary Outwater White, 8 June 1887, DMUA.

9. See *The Diaries of Andrew D. White*, ed. Robert Morris Ogden (Ithaca, 1959).

10. White to Gerrit Smith, 1 Sept. 1862, White papers, DMUA.

11. The early association of these two men and the controversial origins of the university are documented in *Autobiography of Andrew D. White*, I, 295–306.

12. White to George Lincoln Burr and Ernest W. Huffcut, 8 Sept. 1893, and George S. Batchellor to Huffcut, July 1894, in Carl Becker, *Cornell University: Founders and the Founding* (Ithaca, 1943), pp. 172–180, 187–190; both letters document the efforts of Cornell and White in obtaining the charter and the bitter struggle involved. *Autobiography of Andrew D. White*, I, 398, indicates White's reluctance to provoke further difficulty by advocating coeducation at this time and his deliberate choice of the word "person." Cornell wrote a lengthy statement defending himself against the variety of accusations, quoted in Becker, *Cornell University*, pp. 168–170. Under these circumstances, I believe the decision to remain silent on the issue of coeducation at this time was realistic rather than indicative of any lack of commitment to the ideal.

13. An excellent reference on the life of Sage is Anita Shafer Goodstein, *Biography of A Businessman* (Ithaca, 1962).

14. Sage Diary, 10 Oct. 1836, DMUA.

15. Reference to Caroline, Sage Diary, 19 Dec. 1836, and to Lucy, 10 Oct. 1836, DMUA.

16. M. Carey Thomas, "Mr. Sage and Coeducation," *Memorial Exercises in Honor of Henry W. Sage*, 22 Feb. 1898, p. 54, DMUA.

17. Cornell University, *Register, 1869–1870*, p. 17.

18. *Ibid.*, p. 28.

19. *Autobiography of Andrew D. White,* I, 398–399; White to Francis Finch, 6 Dec. 1898, White papers, DMUA.

20. Cornell University, *Proceedings at the Laying of the Cornerstone of Sage College,* 15 May 1873, p. 26. Biographical data in *NAW,* I, 22–25. Elizabeth Agassiz later became president of Radcliffe College.

21. *NAW,* II, 230.

22. Mitchell to Ezra Cornell, 10 March 1868, Cornell papers, DMUA. Biographical data in *NAW,* II, 554–556.

23. *Cornell Era,* 27 March 1869, p. 4; Hewett, *Cornell University,* I, 259–260; and Goldwin Smith to White, 17 Dec. 1883, Smith papers, DMUA. Smith recalled that Cornell "had melted butter poured over his head and down his back by Susan B. Anthony."

24. Biographical data in *NAW,* I, 121–124, and Katherine K. Sklar, *Catharine Beecher: A Study in American Domesticity* (New Haven, 1973).

25. Quoted in Philip Dorf, *The Builder: A Biography of Ezra Cornell* (New York, 1952), p. 373.

26. Sklar, *Catharine Beecher,* p. 258.

27. Catharine Beecher to Andrew D. and Mary White, 11 Aug. 1871, 25 March 1872, 28 March 1872; White papers, DMUA.

Chapter 3. Sage College: Woman's Place at Cornell

1. Newcomer, *A Century of Higher Education,* p. 19.

2. Although many students were attracted by the new mode of education offered at Cornell, others were drawn by the widely publicized proposal that students could earn the cost of their Cornell education through manual labor for the university. Unbeknownst to White, Ezra Cornell wrote to the *New York Tribune,* 15 Aug. 1868, promising paid employment for needy students. This letter caused a deluge of applications and one student even traveled all the way from Russia. The problem of severe overcrowding was compounded by continual delays in the construction of facilities. See *Autobiography of Andrew D. White,* I, 344–346, and Becker, *Cornell University,* pp. 131, 239–240.

3. White to Russel, 7 Dec. 1871, White papers, DMUA.

4. Hewett, *Cornell University,* I, 259.

5. The difficulties of travel in the area of the university are discussed in Kermit Carlyle Parsons, *The Cornell Campus: A History of*

Its Planning and Development (Ithaca, 1968), pp. 94–96, and in Hewett, *Cornell University*, I, 173–174.

6. Elisabeth Wallace, *Goldwin Smith: Victorian Liberal* (Toronto, 1957), pp. 42–49.

7. Reference to Smith's plans to build a house on the campus in Parsons, *The Cornell Campus*, p. 111. Comment about his cremation quoted in Morris Bishop, *A History of Cornell* (Ithaca, 1962), p. 105.

8. Wallace, *Goldwin Smith*, p. 48.

9. Hewett, *Cornell University*, I, 260.

10. Ellen Brown Elliott, "Yesterday," *Cornell Alumni News*, Feb. 1973, p. 27.

11. Henry Randall to White, 9 Sept. 1870, White papers, DMUA.

12. Sage to White, 5 June 1871, Sage papers, DMUA.

13. White to Francis Finch, 6 Dec. 1897, White papers, DMUA.

14. *Cornell Era*, 30 March 1870, p. 196.

15. The following discussion of various coeducational institutions and the arguments analyzing coeducation are taken from Andrew D. White, *A Report Submitted to the Trustees of Cornell University, in Behalf of a Majority of the Committee on Mr. Sage's Proposal to Endow a College for Women*, 13 Feb. 1872, DMUA.

16. Sage to the Trustees of Cornell University, 13 Feb. 1872, DMUA.

17. White to Russel, 15 Feb. 1872, White papers, DMUA.

18. Russel to White, 16 Feb. 1872, White papers, DMUA.

19. Russel to White, 16 Feb. 1872, White papers, DMUA.

20. Martha Goddard to White, 19 May 1872, White papers, DMUA.

21. *Cornell Era*, 2 Feb. 1872, p. 245.

22. For Smith's abandonment of building plans, see Parsons, *The Cornell Campus*, p. 15. Wallace, *Goldwin Smith*, pp. 48–50, discusses the factors in his decision to resign.

23. "The Position of Women as Recently Discussed," *New York Times*, 20 June 1874.

24. Smith's fears that coeducation would cause a loss of public confidence quoted in *Cornell Era*, 19 Sept. 1873, p. 10. Additional objections in letter from Smith to White, 26 July 1870, Smith papers, DMUA.

25. Smith to C. S. Norton, 17 July 1870, quoted in Wallace, *Goldwin Smith*, pp. 48–49.

26. All information about this occasion contained in *Proceedings at the Laying of the Sage Cornerstone*, 15 May 1873, DMUA.

27. Smith to Mrs. Waring, 25 Oct. 1872, quoted in Wallace, *Goldwin Smith*, p. 55. Smith reported that he was participating in a movement "for the intellectual regeneration of that unsatisfactory creature woman" by giving lectures on English history to a ladies' class in Montreal and admitted that the class did "very well."

28. Smith referred to the cancellation of a previous engagement and his great effort to be present to express his steadfast admiration of Ezra Cornell in *Proceedings*, pp. 39–42. In Dorf's *The Builder* (New York, 1952), pp. 407–416, Dorf described the attack on Ezra Cornell, the consternation it caused among those at the university, and the pall this charge cast over the Sage College program. The following day, all classes were suspended so that President White could address the student body to refute the charges.

29. The Sage College Collection contains the original correspondence White had concerning the construction and furnishing of Sage College, DMUA.

30. Information about the advantages of living in Sage College can be found in an undated brochure, *The Sage College at Cornell University*, issued "in response to various inquiries regarding the Sage College for Lady Students at the Cornell University," DMUA.

31. Order for four chairs in the Sage College Collection, DMUA.

32. *The Sage College at Cornell University*, DMUA.

33. Quoted in Albert W. Smith, *Ezra Cornell: A Character Study* (Ithaca, 1934), p. 206.

34. Cornell University, *Register, 1872–1873*, p. 53.

35. Sources of information on individual women are as follows. Comstock: *The Comstocks of Cornell* and *NAW*, I, 367–368. Gage: Memorial booklet in Mary Crawford papers, DMUA; *Cornell Alumni News*, 4 Nov. 1915, pp. 67–68; Margaret Rossiter, "Women Scientists in America before 1920," the *American Scientist*, 62 (May–June 1974), 317. Kelley: Florence Kelley folder DMUA; Josephine Goldmark, *Impatient Crusader: Florence Kelley's Life Story* (Urbana, 1953); *NAW*, II, 316–319. Putnam: Ruth Putnam folder, DMUA. Thomas: Julia Thomas Irvine folder, DMUA. Thomas: Edith Finch, *Carey Thomas of Bryn Mawr* (New York, 1947); *NAW*, III, 446–450; M. Carey Thomas folder, DMUA.

36. Gage: see note 35. Fleming: Edith Fox, "Some Women of

Ithaca," (undated manuscript), Fox papers, DMUA. Gleason: Kate Gleason folder, DMUA; *NAW,* II, 51–52.

37. An excerpt from the Plan of Organization (1866) discusses White's opposition to the dormitory system, quoted in Bishop, *A History,* p. 78.

38. May Preston Slosson folder, DMUA. Interview with Mrs. Slosson included in the Florence Hazzard papers.

39. *NAW,* III, 588–589. Interviews with Agnes Gouinlock Conable '08 (3 Aug. 1973) and Annie Bullivant Pfeiffer '12 (23 March 1976) reflect Helen White's great interest in the women students, her active support of their activities, and her elegant social events in which women students were regularly included.

40. David Lockmiller, *Scholars on Parade* (New York, 1969), p. 218; Walter C. Eells, *Degrees in Higher Education* (Washington, D.C., 1963), p. 41.

41. The establishment of scholarships for women is documented in Hewett, *Cornell University,* I, 159, and in *Sage College for Women* (1884), p. 8, Sage College Collection, DMUA. The socio-economic groups served by the women's colleges is found in Newcomer, *A Century of Higher Education,* pp. 130–131.

42. Bishop, *A History,* p. 244, and Newcomer, *A Century of Higher Education,* pp. 98–99.

43. *A Tribute to Henry W. Sage from the Women Graduates of Cornell University, 1895,* DMUA.

44. See notes 35 and 36.

45. Bishop, *A History,* p. 499.

46. Correspondence between White and Mrs. Sage, White papers, and in the Prudence Risley Log, 8 July 1910 through 4 Feb. 1911, DMUA. White also recorded his concern about the potential Sage gift, and the plans for a second college for women in his diary. See *Diaries of Andrew D. White,* pp. 429–434.

47. Parsons, *The Cornell Campus,* p. 216.

48. The friendship of Sage and Stanton is documented in Alma Lutz, *Created Equal: A Biography of Elizabeth Cady Stanton* (New York, 1940), p. 291, and in Blatch and Stanton, I, 340. In addition to her granddaughter, Nora Blatch, two of Stanton's sons, Robert and Theodore, attended Cornell.

49. In her diary, Stanton first referred to her friend Russell Sage in 1888. On 10 Aug. 1893, she described a visit with Mrs. Sage in which they discussed Cornell. Stanton urged Sage to see that any

contributions her husband might make to Cornell were designated for the women students. On 16 Oct. 1893, they held further conversations about Cornell and coeducation. Stanton recorded that she had converted Sage to the cause of woman suffrage. On 9 Feb. 1895, Stanton learned from Sage of the Schurman request and again urged that gifts to Cornell should benefit only women, not men. Sage agreed. See Blatch and Stanton, II, 295, 298.

Chapter 4. The Education of Womanly Women and Manly Men, 1885–1960

1. *Cornell Era,* 11 Feb. 1876, p. 134.

2. Leonard N. Beck, "The Library of Susan B. Anthony," *Quarterly Journal of the Library of Congress,* 32 (Oct. 1975), 325–335. Also in Lutz, *Susan B. Anthony,* pp. 74–76.

3. The Carnegie Commission on Higher Education, *Opportunities for Women in Higher Education* (New York, 1973), p. 71.

4. Carnegie, *Opportunities,* p. 52.

5. Sage to White, 17 Dec. 1875, Sage papers, DMUA.

6. Comstock, *The Comstocks,* p.80.

7. *Cornell Era,* 2 May 1879, p. 302.

8. Executive Committee Minutes, 20 June 1879, 6 Sept. 1879, DMUA.

9. Moses Coit Tyler Diaries, 12 Jan. 1882, Rare Book Collection, Cornell University Libraries.

10. Ogden, *The Diaries,* pp. 224–225.

11. Sage to Hon. Stewart Woodford, 12 July 1883, and to Mrs. Agnes Derkheim, 16 April 1884, Sage papers, DMUA.

12. *Circular Issued by the Trustees,* July 1884, Sage College Memorial Collection, DMUA.

13. All correspondence related to the regulation of Sage College and the alumnae petition to the Board of Trustees, 9 June 1885, are found in the Sage College Memorial Collection, DMUA; the correspondence includes letters between Brown and White, 17 June–1 Aug. 1884, and letter from the Gages to Stella Spencer and Emma Bassett, 15 June 1884. In a reminiscence of this incident, written in 1935 and included in this collection. Brown recalls the constant support given by White to the women students.

14. White's resignation, although hinted at earlier, came as a surprise at this meeting. In addition, White proposed the immedi-

ate election of his successor, which caused much controversy. See Bishop, *A History*, p. 256. Sage's opposition tabled the petition permanently.

15. *Report of the President, 1890–1891*, pp. 25–28.

16. Bishop, p. 201.

17. *Ibid.*, p. 208.

18. *New York Times*, 27 July 1874.

19. Quoted in Parsons, *The Cornell Campus*, p. 80.

20. Parsons, p. 81.

21. Milton Rugoff, *Prudery and Passion: Sexuality in Victorian America* (New York, 1971), p. 55.

22. In Bishop, *A History*, pp. 214–223, there is evidence of the increasingly heated public debate over Cornell University's lack of traditional religious affiliations, a struggle which resulted in the firing of the vice president and the assertion of Sage as the power on the Board of Trustees. In a letter from Russel to White, 31 Oct. 1880, DMUA, Russel noted Sage's sensitivity on this issue and observed, "Brooklyn orthodoxy, or rather Beecher orthodoxy, is very thin but excessively sensitive to reputation." Susan Sage's disapproval of coeducation noted in Thomas, "Mr. Sage and Coeducation," p. 54.

23. *Report of the Adviser of Women, 1910–1911*, p. lxxvi.

24. Personal study of records of the University Registrar at ten year intervals.

25. Carnegie, *Opportunities*, p. 52.

26. Donna Katherine Barnes, "The Cornell National Scholarships: A Review and Evaluation of the First Ten Years" (unpublished M.A. thesis, Cornell University, 1954), p. 67.

27. *Registrar's Report, 1950–1951*, p. 50.

28. Jennie T. Farley, "Women on the March Again: The Rebirth of Feminism in an Academic Community" (unpublished Ph.D. dissertation, Cornell University, 1970), p. 57.

29. Personal study.

30. The growth of the student body in Bishop, *A History*, pp. 352–353; the proportion of females calculated by personal study.

31. "Coeducation at Cornell," *New York Herald*, 24 June 1894, DMUA.

32. The intensity of anticoedism was variable according to the specific fraternities and colleges. While the elite fraternities and some professional colleges promoted this tradition with vigor, it

had less impact in units like the College of Agriculture and among students living off campus.

33. Gertrude Nelson to her parents, 1 Oct. 1892, DMUA.

34. Bishop, *A History*, p. 498.

35. *Cornell Era*, 21 Feb. 1879, p. 207.

36. *Ibid.*, 28 Feb. 1879, p. 222.

37. *Ibid.*, 7 March 1879, p. 234.

38. Board of Trustees, "Memorial Resolution for Dr. Mary Crawford," Jan. 1973. The opinions expressed in *Cornell Era*, Nov. 1900, pp. 99–102, and Oct. 1900, pp. 76–79.

39. Katherine Kirk Thornton, "Women at Cornell: A Problem in Minority Group Relations" (paper for Sociology 385 class, Cornell University, 29 May 1951), p. 10.

40. Bessie D. Beahan to Dr. Mary Crawford, 7 Dec. 1936, Mary Crawford papers, DMUA.

41. Quoted from personal survey.

42. Rose K. Goldsen et al., *What College Students Think* (New York, 1960), pp. 81–83. This study, which includes Cornell men and women, referred to student concerns over the formality, artificiality, and competitiveness of the campus social life. In the reports of discussion groups at the Student Council Workshop on Campus Affairs, Oct. 1949, concern was expressed over the highly structured, formal nature of campus social life and the unmet social needs of students.

43. Matina Horner, in "Woman's Will to Fail," *Psychology Today*, Nov. 1969, suggests the conflict between achievement and femininity which women often experience in competition with men and the lowering of achievement motivation which frequently results. At Cornell, this effect would be intensified by the placing of a small number of highly intelligent women in a largely male environment with intense social pressure.

44. Thornton, "Women at Cornell," pp. 6–7. Editorials in the *Cornell Daily Sun* advocated election of women to offices in student government in 1945.

45. M. Elizabeth Tidball, "Perspective on Academic Women and Affirmative Action," *Educational Record*, 54 (Spring 1973), 130–135.

46. Ezra Cornell to Marietta Parker, 28 April 1874, Cornell papers, DMUA.

47. Flora Rose et al., *A Growing College: Home Economics at Cornell University* (Ithaca, 1969), pp. 36–37.

48. Personal survey, *University Register*, 1898–1972.

49. Margaret W. Rossiter, "Women Scientists in America before 1920,"*American Scientist*, 62 (1974), 319.

50. Rossiter, p. 315; Elizabeth Tidball and Vera Kistiakowsky, "Baccalaureate Origins of American Scientists and Scholars," *Science*, 193 (1976), 646–652.

51. Interview, 28 Oct. 1976.

52. Report from Joyce Cima to Charlotte Conable on the women who have served on the Board of Trustees, July 1973.

53. Dr. Mary Crawford to Bessie D. Beahan, 3 June 1937, Crawford papers, DMUA.

54. Cima report.

55. *Report of the Adviser of Women, 1911–1912*, quoted in Bishop, *A History*, p. 420.

56. See the following studies: Carnegie, *Opportunities;* Tidball, "Perspective on Academic Women"; Horner, "Woman's Will to Fail"; and Ruth Oltman, *Campus 1970: Where Do Women Stand?* (Washington, 1970). In summary, these studies indicate that Cornell University contains most of the factors which militate against the fullest development of female ability, such as a research orientation, particularly in science; it is a large coeducational institution, has a high ratio of men to women and a lack of female role models; and social pressure is intense.

57. Bishop, *A History*, p. 498.

Epilogue

1. *Cornell Era*, 13 Oct. 1871, p. 55.

2. The pervasiveness of sex bias in research and educational programs has been thoroughly documented in recent years and is the causal factor in the development of women's studies. Among the first to publicize the extensive influence of sex-biased education were Betty Friedan, *The Feminine Mystique* (New York, 1964) and Alice S. Rossi, "Equality between the Sexes: An Immodest Proposal" in Robert Jay Lifton, ed., *The Woman in America* (Boston, 1964), pp. 98–143.

3. Thorstein Veblen, *The Theory of the Leisure Class* (New York, 1899).

4. The effect of educational attention to the special needs of

women, changing mores, and the Depression in encouraging revitalization of domestic goals for women is discussed in William H. Chafe, *The American Woman: Her Changing Social, Economic, and Political Roles, 1920–1970* (New York, 1972), pp. 89–111. A classic argument for the rejection of male-oriented coeducational institutions and the development of programs to meet the special needs of women is presented in Lynn White, Jr., *Educating Our Daughters: A Challenge to the Colleges* (New York, 1950).

5. Leonard K. Elmhirst, "The Place on the Hill," *Cornell Alumni News*, Oct. 1975, pp. 22–23.

6. *Cornell Alumni News*, Oct. 1975, pp. 15–27; Thornton, "Women at Cornell," p. 9.

7. Quoted from personal survey.

8. Recollection of Colin G. Campbell '57 of fraternity life 1953–1957. Campbell to Conable, 21 Aug. 1974.

9. Sheila Tobias, "Sex, Politics, and the New Feminism," *Cornell Alumni News*, May 1970, p. 20.

10. Farley, "Women on the March Again," pp. 47–63. Throughout her thesis, Farley documents the origins of feminism at Cornell in the 1960s. The radical women believed themselves mistreated in leftist groups like the SDS while conservative older women on the right felt they were being unfairly excluded from jobs.

11. *Ibid.*, p. 14.

12. Charlotte Conable, "Women, Affirmative Action, and Cornell University" (term paper, Women's Studies 240, George Washington University, April 1975). Although I believe federal affirmative action is extremely beneficial in establishing the legal principle of equality, its impact upon this institution has been limited. The Affirmative Action Office was poorly designed for effective data gathering and lacked the leverage to press for change, a process complicated by the complexity of the institution. There is, in addition, a longstanding tradition of power vested in deans, faculty, and the various colleges which relates directly to issues of employment. There is resistance in some groups to the compilation of necessary data and the revision of traditional search procedures. Government actions have served only to intensify this negativism by the continual revision of ambiguous regulations.

13. Women's Studies Program, "Women's Studies at Cornell University: Eight Questions Answered," 12 Sept. 1975 (mimeographed).

14. Report of the Ad Hoc Trustee Committee on the Status of Women, *A Commitment to Equality: One Century Later,* table 7.

15. Provost's Advisory Committee on the Status of Women, Fall 1976.

16. Cornell Women's Caucus, "Report on the Status of Women at Cornell," Feb. 1976, pp. 14–17 (mimeographed).

17. The dramatic increase of women on the board is the result of several factors. Following the disruptions of the 1960s, a new campus governing body was formed in 1970 with the power to elect nine representatives to the board from the faculty, the student body, and the outside community. Four of these are women. The faculty itself recently elected a woman. The lieutenant governor of the State of New York, an ex-officio member, is a woman. The alumni are now more supportive of women candidates, and three have been elected in recent successive years. The terms of office vary according to the constituency. As of March 1977, the system of campus governance has undergone drastic revision, students have lost the power to elect one faculty member to the Board, and the outcome of future elections of trustees by students is unpredictable. The term of a woman elected by the faculty expires and no woman has been nominated by the alumni this year.

18. Provost's Advisory Committee, Fall 1976.

19. Provost's Advisory Committee, Fall 1976.

20. Alice S. Rossi, "Summary and Prospects," in Alice S. Rossi and Ann Calderwood, eds., *Academic Women on the Move* (New York, 1973), pp. 506–510.

21. Letter from Professor and Mrs. Simon H. Gage to Stella Spencer and Emma Bassett, 15 July 1884, Sage College Memorial Collection, DMUA.

Selected Bibliography

Unpublished sources about Cornell: Letters, Papers, Theses

Items located in the Department of Manuscripts and University Archives, Cornell University Libraries are identified by the abbreviation DMUA.

Barnes, Donna K. "Cornell National Scholarships: Evaluation of the First Ten Years." M.A. thesis, Cornell University, 1954.

Bergen, Carolyn J. "A Study of Environmental Press among Selected Women Undergraduate Groups at Cornell University." M.A. thesis, Cornell University, 1964.

Conable, Charlotte W. "Elizabeth Cady Stanton 1818–1902: Portrait of a New Yorker." Term project, Women's Studies 221, George Washington University, April 1974.

——. "Woman's Work in Woman's Place: An Analysis of the Home Economics Profession." Term project, Women's Studies 260, George Washington University, Dec. 1975.

——. "Women, Affirmative Action, and Cornell University." Term project, Women's Studies 240, George Washington University, April 1975.

——. "Women in Higher Education: Does Sex Make a Difference?" Term project, Sociology 191, George Washington University, Nov. 1973.

Cornell, Ezra. Letters, 1843–1874. DMUA.

Cornell Student Council. "Reports of Discussion Groups at the Student Council Workshop on Campus Affairs." 15 and 16 Oct. 1949. (Mimeographed.)

Cornell Women's Caucus. "Report on the Status of Women at Cornell." Feb. 1976. (Mimeographed.)

Crawford, Caroline. Papers, 1895–1906. DMUA.

Crawford, Mary Merritt. Papers, 1903–1937. DMUA.

Farley, Jennie T. "Women on the March Again: The Rebirth of Feminism in an Academic Community." Ph.D. dissertation, Cornell University, 1970.

Fox, Edith M. Papers, 1870–1885. DMUA.

Freeman, Ruth St. John. Scrapbook, Class of 1922. DMUA.

Haines, Patricia. "Women, Men, and Coeducation: Historical Perspectives from Cornell University 1868–1900." Paper presented at the Berkshire Women's History Conference at Bryn Mawr, Pa., June 1976.

Hazzard, Florence W. Papers, undated collection. DMUA.

Millet, Kate. "Sex, Politics, and the New Feminism." Lecture at Cornell University, 13 Nov. 1968.

Nelson, Gertrude. Letters, 1891–1897. DMUA.

People's College Collection. 1851–1886. DMUA.

Petition to Cornell University from the Cornell Women's Club of New York City. May 1913. DMUA.

Prudence Risley Hall Collection. 1910–1925. DMUA.

Richardson, Barbara Francis. "The Status of Women at Cornell." Sept. 1969. (Mimeographed.)

Sage College Collection. 1871–1885. DMUA.

Sage, Henry W. Papers, 1836–1895. DMUA.

Schurman, Jacob Gould. Papers, 1893–1920. DMUA.

Smith, Donald. "The Origin and Early Years of Coeducation at Cornell University." Paper presented in competition for the Knoblaugh Prize, 14 April 1955. DMUA.

Smith, Goldwin. Letters, 1870–1883. DMUA.

Stebbins, Linda B. "An Exploratory Study of the Roles of Certain Students, Faculty, and Administrators as Perceived by Undergraduate Women at Cornell University." M.A. thesis, Cornell University, 1967.

Taber, Adelaide Young. Letters, 1895–1896. DMUA.

Thornton, Katherine Kirk. "Women at Cornell: A Problem in Minority Group Relations." Paper for Sociology 385, Cornell University, 29 May 1951.

White, Andrew Dickson. Letters, 1862–1911. DMUA.

Women's Sage College Memorial Collection. 1884–1885. DMUA.

Women's Self Government Association Collection. 1915–1968. DMUA.

Zehler, Cornelia. Letters, 1913–1914. DMUA.

Zeller, Adelheid. Papers, 1911–1916. DMUA.

Cornell and Cornellians: Books, Newspapers, Periodicals, Records

Barringer, Emily Dunning. *From Bowery to Bellevue.* New York: Norton, 1950.

Becker, Carl. *Cornell University: Founders and the Founding.* Ithaca: Cornell University Press, 1943.

Bishop, Morris. *A History of Cornell.* Ithaca: Cornell University Press, 1962.

Colman, Gould P. *Education and Agriculture: A History of the New York State College of Agriculture at Cornell University.* Ithaca: Cornell University, 1963.

Comstock, Anna Botsford. *The Comstocks of Cornell.* Ithaca: Comstock Publishing Co., 1953.

Cornell, Alonzo. *True and Firm: A Biography of Ezra Cornell.* New York: Barnes, 1884.

Cornell, Mary Emily. *The Autobiography of Mary Emily Cornell.* Ithaca: Cayuga Press, 1929.

Cornell Alumni News. 1920–1977.

Cornell Chronicle. 1971–1977.

Cornell Daily Sun. 1947–1977.

——. *A Half Century at Cornell, 1880–1930.* Ithaca: Cayuga Press, 1930.

——. *Name Withheld: Previously Published Articles and Hitherto Unpublished Correspondence to the Editor of the Sun on the Question of the Ratio of the Cornell Male to the Cornell Female.* April 1950.

Cornell Era. 1868–1900.

Cornell University. *A Commitment to Equality: One Century Later.* Report of the Ad Hoc Trustee Committee on the Status of Women. March 1974.

——. *Account of the Proceedings at the Inauguration.* 7 Oct. 1868. DMUA.

——. Annual Reports. Office of the Registrar. 1961–1977.

——. *Memorial Exercises in Honor of Henry W. Sage.* 1898. DMUA.

——. *Proceedings at the Laying of the Cornerstone of Sage College.* 15 May 1873. DMUA.

——. *Proceedings of the Board of Trustees.* April 1865–July 1885. DMUA.

——. *Register.* 1868–1974.

——. *Report of the President.* 1883–1974.

——. *Report of the Trustees in Behalf of a Majority of the Committee on Mr. Sage's Proposal to Endow a College for Women.* Albany, N.Y.: 13 Feb. 1872. DMUA.

Dallenbach, Karl M. "Margaret Floy Washburn, 1871–1939." *American Journal of Psychology,* 53 (Jan. 1940), 1–5.

Dorf, Philip. *The Builder: A Biography of Ezra Cornell.* New York: Macmillan, 1952.

Finch, Edith. *Carey Thomas of Bryn Mawr.* New York: Harper, 1947.

Goldmark, Josephine. *Impatient Crusader: Florence Kelley's Life Story.* Urbana: University of Illinois Press, 1953.

Goldsen, Rose K.; Morris Rosenberg; Robin M. Williams; and Edward A. Suchman. *What College Students Think.* New York: D. Van Nostrand, 1960.

Goodstein, Anita Shafer. *Biography of a Businessman.* Ithaca: Cornell University Press, 1962.

Hewett, Waterman T. *Cornell University: A History.* 4 vols. New York: The University Publishing Society, 1905.

Howes, Raymond F., ed. *Our Cornell.* Ithaca: Cornell Alumni Association, 1939.

Kelley, Florence. "When Coeducation Was Young." *Survey,* 1 Feb. 1927, 557–602.

Lindy, Elaine. *Woman's Roots: The History of Women in Tompkins County.* Ithaca: Home Town Publications, 1976.

Macklin, Eleanor D. "Cohabitation in College: Going Very Steady." *Psychology Today,* Nov. 1974, pp. 53–59.

Ogden, Robert Morris, ed. *The Diaries of Andrew D. White.* Ithaca: Cornell University Library, 1959.

Parsons, Kermit Carlyle. *The Cornell Campus: A History of Its Planning and Development.* Ithaca: Cornell University Press, 1968.

Percival, Caroline M. *Martha Van Rensselaer.* Ithaca: Alumnae Association, New York State College of Home Economics, Cornell University, 1957.

Rose, Flora; Esther H. Stocks; and Michael W. Whittier. *A Growing College: Home Economics at Cornell University.* Ithaca: Cornell University, 1969.

Slosson, Edwin E. *Great American Universities*. New York: Macmillan, 1910.

Smith, Albert W. *Ezra Cornell: A Character Study*. Ithaca: Wm. A. Church, 1934.

The Cornellian. 1925–1975.

Tobias, Sheila; Ella Kusnetz; and Deborah Spitz, eds. *Proceedings of the Cornell Conference on Women, 22–25 Jan. 1969*. Pittsburgh, Pa.: KNOW, INC., 1969.

Tribute to Henry W. Sage from the Women Graduates of Cornell University. Ithaca: 1895. DMUA.

Wallace, Elisabeth. *Goldwin Smith: Victorian Liberal*. Toronto: University of Toronto Press, 1957.

White, Andrew D. *The Autobiography of Andrew D. White*. New York: Century, 1905; rpt. 1932.

General References

Baine, E. V. "Women Holders of Leadership Positions on the Coeducational Campus." *Journal of the National Association of Women Deans, Administrators, and Counsellors*, 32 (1968), 39–40.

Baker, Liva. "The 'Seven Sisters' Are Celebrating Their Centenaries." *Smithsonian Magazine*, Feb. 1974, pp. 82–88.

Blatch, Harriot S., and Theodore Stanton, eds. *Elizabeth Cady Stanton as Revealed in Her Letters, Diary, and Reminiscences*. 2 vols. New York: Harper, 1922.

Carnegie Commission on Higher Education. *Opportunities for Women in Higher Education*. New York: McGraw-Hill, 1973.

Chafe, William H. *The American Woman: Her Changing Social, Economic, and Political Roles, 1920–1970*. New York: Oxford University Press, 1972.

Chronicle of Higher Education. 1974–1977.

Clarke, Edward. *Sex in Education or a Fair Chance for Girls*. 1873; rpt. New York: Arno Press, 1972.

Conway, Jill K. "Coeducation and Women's Studies: Two Approaches to the Question of Women's Place in the Contemporary University." *Daedalus*, 1 (1974), 239–249.

Cross, Whitney R. *The Burned-Over District: The Social and Intellectual History of Enthusiastic Religion in Western New York, 1800–1850*. Ithaca: Cornell University Press, 1950.

Eells, Walter C. *Degrees in Higher Education.* Washington, D.C.: Center for Applied Research in Education, 1963.

Flexner, Eleanor. *Century of Struggle: The Woman's Rights Movement in the United States.* 1959; rpt. New York: Atheneum, 1972.

Fley, Jo Ann. "The Time to Be Properly Vicious." *Journal of the National Association of Women Deans, Administrators, and Counsellors,* 37 (1974), 53–58.

Friedan, Betty. *The Feminine Mystique.* New York: Dell, 1963.

Gemmell, Suzanne. "The Affirmative Action Officer." *Journal of the National Association of Women Deans, Administrators, and Counsellors,* 38 (1975), 87–92.

Harkness, Georgia E. *Women in Church and Society: A Historical and Theological Inquiry.* Nashville.: Abingdon Press, 1972.

Harlow, Ralph V. *Gerrit Smith: Philanthropist and Reformer.* New York: Russell and Russell, 1972.

Hole, Judith, and Ellen Levine. *Rebirth of Feminism.* New York: Quadrangle Books, 1971.

Holmes, Peter. "Affirmative Action: Myth and Reality." Speech delivered to the American Political Science Association, Sept. 1973.

Horner, Matina S. "Woman's Will to Fail." *Psychology Today,* November 1969, pp. 36–38, 62.

James, Edward T., and Janet Wilson James, eds. *Notable American Women, 1607–1950: A Biographical Dictionary.* 3 vols. Cambridge, Mass.: Belknap Press of Harvard University, 1971.

Kass, Alvin. *Politics in New York State, 1800–1830.* Syracuse: Syracuse University Press, 1965.

Klafs, Carl E., and M. Joan Lyon. *The Female Athlete: Conditioning, Competition, and Culture.* Saint Louis: Mosby, 1973.

Kundsin, Ruth B., ed. *Women and Success: The Anatomy of Achievement.* New York: Morrow, 1974.

Leppaluoto, Jean R. "Attitude Change and Sex Discrimination: The Crunch Hypothesis." Paper presented before the Western Psychological Association, 1972. ERIC Reports ED 071 548. Washington, D.C.: Office of Education, 1972.

Lifton, Robert J., ed. *The Woman in America.* Boston: Beacon Press, 1964.

Lockmiller, David A. *Scholars on Parade.* New York: Macmillan, 1969.

Lutz, Alma. *Created Equal: A Biography of Elizabeth Cady Stanton, 1815–1902.* New York: Day, 1940.

———. *Susan B. Anthony: Rebel, Crusader, Humanitarian.* Boston: Beacon Press, 1959.

Massey, Mary Elizabeth. *Bonnet Brigades.* Impact of the Civil War Series. New York: Knopf, 1966.

Mattfeld, Jacquelyn A. "Many Are Called but Few Are Chosen." Paper about women administrators at Ivy League institutions, presented at the annual meeting of the American Council on Education, 6 Oct. 1972. ERIC Reports ED 071 549. Washington, D.C.: Office of Education, 1972.

———, and Carol G. VanAken, eds. *Women and the Scientific Professions: The MIT Symposium on American Women in Science and Engineering.* Cambridge, Mass.: M.I.T. Press, 1965.

McGuigan, Dorothy G. *The Dangerous Experiment: 100 Years of Women at the University of Michigan.* Ann Arbor: Center for the Continuing Education for Women, 1970.

Melder, Keith. "Mask of Oppression: The Female Seminary Movement in the United States." *New York History,* 55 (1974), 261–279.

Mill, John Stuart, and Harriet Taylor Mill. *Essays on Sex Equality.* Ed. Alice S. Rossi. Chicago: University of Chicago Press, 1970.

Miller, Douglas. *Jacksonian Aristocracy: Class and Democracy in New York, 1830–1860.* New York: Oxford University Press, 1967.

Mumford, Thomas J., ed. *Memoir of Samuel J. May.* Boston: Roberts Bros., 1873.

Newcomer, Mabel. *A Century of Higher Education for American Women.* New York: Harper, 1959.

O'Brien, Gael. "Male Professors Found Cool to Women's Issues." *Chronicle of Higher Education,* 5 April 1976, p. 8.

Oltman, Ruth M. *Campus 1970: Where Do Women Stand?* Washington, D.C.: American Association of University Women, 1970.

O'Neill, William L. *Everyone Was Brave: A History of Feminism in America.* Chicago: Quadrangle Books, 1971.

Project on the Status and Education of Women. *Federal Laws and Regulations Concerning Sex Discrimination in Educational Institutions.* Washington, D.C.: Association of American Colleges, 1975.

Rich, Adrienne C. "Toward a Woman-Centered University." *Chronicle of Higher Education,* 21 July 1975, p. 32.

Robinson, Lora. *Women's Studies: Courses and Programs for Higher Education.* Washington, D.C.: American Association for Higher Education, 1973.

Rossi, Alice S., and Ann Calderwood, eds. *Academic Women on the Move.* New York: Russell Sage Foundation, 1973.

Rossiter, Margaret W. "Women Scientists in America before 1920." *American Scientist,* 62 (1974), 312–323.

Rugoff, Milton. *Prudery and Passion: Sexuality in Victorian America.* New York: Putnam, 1971.

Sandler, Bernice. "What Constitutes Equity for Women in Higher Education?" Address presented at Concurrent General Session I of the 27th National Conference on Higher Education, 7 March 1972. ERIC Reports ED 061 870. Washington, D.C.: Office of Education, 1972.

——. "Women in Higher Education: A Progress Report." *AAUW Journal,* (November 1973), 17–22.

Sklar, Katherine K. *Catharine Beecher: A Study in American Domesticity.* New Haven: Yale University Press, 1973.

Smuts, Robert W. *Women and Work in America.* Studies in the Life of Women Series. New York: Schocken Books, 1971.

Stanton, Elizabeth Cady. *Eighty Years and More: Reminiscences, 1815–1897.* 1898; rpt. New York: Schocken Books, 1971.

Stanton, Elizabeth Cady; Susan B. Anthony; Matilda J. Gage; and Ida H. Harper, eds. *History of Woman Suffrage.* 6 vols. New York: Fowler and Wells, 1881–1922.

Talbot, Marion, and Lois Kimball Mathews Rosenberry. *The History of the American Association of University Women, 1881–1931.* New York: Houghton Mifflin, 1931.

Tidball, M. Elizabeth. "Perspective on Academic Women and Affirmative Action." *Educational Record,* 54 (1973), 130–135.

——, and Vera Kistiakowsky. "Baccalaureate Origins of American Scientists and Scholars." *Science,* 193 (1976), 646–652.

Tyler, Alice Felt. *Freedom's Ferment: Phases of American Social History from the Colonial Period to the Outbreak of the Civil War.* 1944; rpt. New York: Harper Torchbooks, 1962.

U.S. Commission on Civil Rights. *The Federal Civil Rights Enforcement Effort-1974: Vol. III-To Ensure Equal Educational Opportunity.* Washington, D.C.: GPO, 1975.

U.S. Congress. Committee on Education and Labor, Special Subcommittee on Education. *Discrimination Against Women.* Hearing, 91st Congress, Second Session, 1 and 31 July, 1970. Washington, D.C.: GPO, 1970.

U.S. Department of Health, Education, and Welfare. "Memorandum to College and University Presidents." Dec. 1974. (Mimeographed.)

——. *Elimination of Sex Discrimination in Athletic Programs.* Washington, D.C.: GPO, 1975.

——. *Higher Education Guidelines: Executive Order 11246.* Washington, D.C.: GPO, 1972.

U.S. Department of Labor. *Trends in the Educational Attainment of Women.* Washington, D.C.: GPO, 1969.

White, Lynn, Jr. *Educating Our Daughters: A Challenge to the Colleges.* New York: Harper, 1950.

Woody, Thomas. *A History of Women's Education in the United States.* 2 vols. New York: The Science Press, 1929.

Zanna, Mark B. "Intellectual Competition and the Female Student." ERIC Reports ED 072 389. Washington, D.C.: Office of Education, 19 Jan. 1973.

Index

Library of Congress Cataloging in Publication Data
(For library cataloging purposes only)

Conable, Charlotte Williams, 1929–
    Women at Cornell.

    Bibliography: p. 197
    Includes index.
    1. Cornell University—Students.   2. Higher education of women—
United States—History.   I. Title.
LD1368.C66   378.747′71   77-3117
ISBN 0-8014-1098-3
ISBN 0-8014-9167-3 pbk.